MW00474767

'This is an ███████████ lightly. Elizab ███████████
her journey to freedom extremely well in this intriguing narrative of growing up in a sect that claims to be God's only right way. This unique and fascinating true story provides a revealing glimpse into a nameless worldwide home church.'

'Reading this book brought tears, smiles and thankfulness for what I consider is a book that everyone should read. It is so well written and holds your interest throughout. It is a book that should be made available to every person who is currently part of this group, anyone considering fellowship with them, or anyone who has never heard of this church which claims to have no name. I wish it had been available many years ago as I think it would have changed the course of my life ... but then I wouldn't have known so many dear people who have experienced more difficulties than I, and are rejoicing today as ex-Two-by-Twos.'

'Elizabeth Coleman writes a fresh and clear description of her spiritual journey from growing up in a family that had long religious connections with the sect variously known in the USA, Australia, and other countries as 'The Way', 'The Church', 'The Two-by-Twos', and also by other names internationally.

A carefully structured juxtaposition between the preachers' teachings and Elizabeth's belief in her right to question them demonstrates the courageous pathway she took as a young adult when she chose to challenge them.

Release from the shattering heritage of workers' influence on her mind and spirit opened the way to joy in belief in Jesus Christ as Saviour but she wisely notes that with separation from the fellowship, time for recovery and healing from embedded beliefs was needed.

This brave work reveals the true colours of the power to silence that preachers believe they hold over quietly obedient members of the fellowship. I recommend this book to any reader interested in the 'Two-by-Two' fellowship, and also in the practise of conditioning of cult or sect members.'

Helen Parker, co-author with Doug Parker of The Secret Sect

Cult to Christ

The Church With No Name and the Legacy of the Living Witness Doctrine

A journey out of spiritual bondage

Elizabeth Coleman

Second Edition October 2015

First published in April 2015 by Adeline Press
PO Box 199 Woden ACT 2606   Australia

Contact: adelinepress@gmail.com

Website: www.culttochristbook.com

Online photos available at Facebook:
www.facebook.com/pages/Elizabeth-Coleman-Cult-to-Christ-
Book/1422568694725497

ISBN 978 0 9942953 0 9

Also available in Kindle, iBook, eBook
ISBN 978 0 9942953 1 6

Front cover (clockwise from top left):
- Convention tents in New South Wales, Australia (as known by the author and still
  currently in use in Australia today);
- The author at 19 years of age (1993), photograph by Cheryl Harriss
- Current portrait (2014) of the author, photograph by David Coleman

Introduction / Explanatory Notes

This book records my experiences concerning a worldwide religious organisation that declines to give itself a name. Members of this group recognise each other by the terms workers (clergy) and friends (lay members). Members refer to their own religious order by the following terms interchangeably: The Way, The Truth, The Meetings, The Fellowship. Former members now most frequently identify this organisation by the term 'Two-by-Twos'. In this account, I refer to the organisation interchangeably as The Meetings, The Friends, The Fellowship or the Two-by-Twos.

This book attempts to be a true record of events. I acknowledge that the version of events recorded here is primarily from my own perspective. Real names have been used for all persons mentioned who are no longer - or who have never been - a part of The Fellowship, unless to do so would be a significant breach of their privacy. Where names have been changed, it is clearly noted. Names of friends, relatives and workers still within The Fellowship have not been used, both for reasons of privacy and to acknowledge that their input or verification has not been sought for the events recorded in this book.

Every attempt has been made to convey events as they occurred. Private conversations are expressed as accurately as can be recalled, and seek to retain the words and intent of the speakers as closely as possible.

Where certain words or phrases appear in italics as part of the general text, this denotes the introduction into the book of a common phraseology used within the group, seeking to familiarise the reader with common verbal and cultural aspects of speech.

I commonly refer herein to the Two-by-Twos as a cult. I know that some may take exception to this label. However, they may also be surprised to learn that the Two-by-Twos are already listed as a cult on numerous cult-identification internet sites (see below). When weighed against the general hallmarks of a cult, the Two-by-Twos fit the **criteria of a Christian cult**; that is, a group which claims to be a Christian group, yet teaches something that is not primarily a Christian belief, or does not align with the historical tenets of the Christian faith. If you are offended by this label, I invite you to undertake further investigation for yourself.

Online Cult Awareness / Research Organisations:
These websites identify the Two-by-Twos as a cult; note that this list is far from exhaustive.

www.apologeticsindex.org

www.caic.org.au (Cult Awareness & Information Centre)

www.carm.org (Christian Apologetics & Research Ministries)

www.neirr.org (New England Institute of Religious Research)

www.mmoutreachinc.com/cult_groups/2x2.html

www.SO4J.com (Sold Out for Jesus)

www.watchman.org (Index of Cults and Religions)

www.cults.co.nz (Cults in New Zealand)

Contents

... on the earth again, like a felled tree sprouting. Something old is being born! We follow the Old and New Testaments, but in a new and living way. It is a life together, something that costs you everything to get, but it is so worth it.

... began from a few people with childlike hearts who left the popular culture of the world, walking away from their old lives. At that time it was mainly young single people, but soon there were families with children, and even grandparents.

According to ... the Son of God, there is a broad gate and a narrow gate, a broad way and a narrow way. He said that only a few would find the narrow way, and that most would prefer the broad way, which leads to death. The narrow way leads to life, but few will travel on it to its destiny. Most are unwilling to pay the high cost of love.

... We make no apology for our way of life. We believe it to be the best thing on earth, and we are all so grateful to live this way.

No, the above quotes do not come from anybody within or associated with the Two-by-Twos (friends and workers), about whom this book is written. Yet the language will be eerily familiar to anyone who has ever been associated with the Two-by-Twos. These quotes come from a group called *The Twelve Tribes* (www.twelvetribes.org), whose doctrine appears similar in many ways to the Two-by-Twos. Both groups have much in common with countless other exclusive religious sects who claim superiority over all other churches and may even actively condition their members against other Christians. This book tells the inside story from just one of many such groups.

A Funeral
February 2012

Jesus said to her, 'I am the resurrection and the life. He who believes in me will live, even though he dies; and whoever lives and believes in me will never die. Do you believe this?'

- John 11:25-26 (NIV)

We laid Papa to rest on a bright, sunny day in early February. Scheduled for mid-morning, we would avoid the later crescendo of inevitable stifling summer heat so familiar to this dry inland city of Wagga Wagga, where my grandparents had lived out their retirement. The funeral directors had set up a marquee as shade for the graveside service, with seating for the family. I sat in the third row, behind his children in the first row and their spouses in the second. I, his eldest grandchild, soaking tissue after tear-stained tissue over the man who had become increasingly distant from me over the past twenty years. The man, who in my childhood, had spent hours telling me stories, playing board games of Chinese checkers and draughts, never letting me win in order to test my true skill. It was enough for me, and him, that I could be an almost worthy opponent. All that was before I grew up and left The Meetings.

Earlier, we grandchildren had formed a guard of honour as the coffin passed by towards its final resting place. The same grave that had already been Nana's for the past eight years, almost to the day. What a diverse group we are, this third generation of the recently deceased. Especially my closer family. My first sister-in-law in her sleeveless, knee-length tailored charcoal dress. My more recently acquired Sydney sister-in-law, tall and elegant, her upper arms wreathed in tattoos peeking out beneath her dark capped sleeves. Me, in a sleeveless knee-length dress, gazing downwards towards my open-toed sandals with painted toenails. Just a few of my many cousins have become 'outsiders', including my funky cousin beside me. Her stylish short hair wisps about her jaw and she wears leggings under her cropped skirt. The descriptions sound ordinary, but we are the outsiders here, significantly at odds with the majority of our relatives and the larger group that stands at a respectful distance, the chasm dividing us much deeper and broader than the open grave between us. The women with their long skirts and bunned hair, shunning makeup and jewellery, are a strange vision of uniformity against the cacophony of our 'worldliness'. My mother is the only rebel in her row, her bob-cropped hair sitting jauntily in defiance of the upswept buns of her sisters and her brother's wives. She even wears a discreet chain and pendant.

My mother is the eldest of seven siblings, and the only one of them to have left The Meetings. I know she debated with her father long and hard about faith. Her faith, his faith, the gospel of the Bible. And now I hear the echo of his voice, a response he'd made to my mother years ago during one of their many discussions which nearly always resulted in an emotionally escalated argument.

'Do you really think I'd be stupid enough to listen to you? To listen to my own daughter, like you have done, and go off and follow other gods?'

Did he know I could hear him that day? I don't know. But the memory of it fans an ember deep in my soul, and my grief is tainted with a burning anger. At all of it. The rules, the system, the lies. Especially the lies. The lies told to my family by these *servants of God,* the *workers*. Yet they, too, are victims of the system. This system, built on a foundation of deception, which continues to uphold a false spiritual authority.

My own hair sits in shoulder length unruly curls, layers freeing it from its former waist-length weight. It – along with dark sunglasses - gives me anonymity for a while, for many at the funeral do not initially recognise me. We exchange pleasantries afterwards, faces familiar to me but names long forgotten. They are part of a former life, a world that continues to turn without me. It strikes me that I have changed as much as they have not. Each one of them is an exact replica of themselves from twenty years prior - the same hair and dress styles - just add aged skin and greying hair. My own mother stands in bright contrast to their faded appearance, her short darkened hair and fashionably clothed lithe figure belying her sixty-odd years. Her freedom from the mental constraints of the group seems somehow reflected in her age-defying appearance.

The external façade of the group is a truly bizarre time warp. Not just from twenty years ago, but actually one hundred and twenty years ago, when this religious order was established in the late 1890s. At a time in society when most women wore buns, they set in place their rigid rules and traditions and from that foundation firmly refused to budge. This particular hairstyle has now been elevated to the status of spiritual necessity within the group; a darkly humorous insight into the fundamental nature of a cult. Not that most of them even know what happened in the 1890s. Those of us who acknowledge the past and speak of it are branded as troublemakers and traitors.

At the graveside, these current-day faithful stalwarts now eye me inquisitively, but direct their greatest curiosity towards my sisters-in-law, whom they have never seen, and who have never been a part of their world. I try to place myself back in the shoes of these watchful but polite people - *the professing* - and see myself through their eyes – one who *gave the devil a foothold* and *lost out of the faith*. Truth be told, I never thought I'd find myself on this side of the chasm.

A light lunch is served back at the family home, many aunts and cousins having spent hours preparing sandwiches, scones and slices. The anguish of it becomes real here, as we face the shell of a home now devoid of its long occupying souls. The familiar landscape of furniture, photos and ornaments make their last brave stand before the final defeat to come - the dismantling and dividing of the earthly remnants of a past generation. None of us can face that today. We want to be comforted by the familiar, and hold on just a little longer.

Much of the extended family is here, as well as many other faithful adherents of The Meetings, including a number who have travelled significant distances. There are four workers present, all male. These spiritual leaders of the group make up its ministry of celibate, homeless preachers, *living by faith*. They are always treated with great respect and deference, but I am long past kowtowing to them. On a sideboard in the family lounge room where we mourners gather is a framed collection of worker photos. A shrine, as I view it, of my grandparents' lifelong devotion and support to these *servants of God*. The adulation of these ordinary faulty humans now irritates me immensely, and I resolve to talk to them as the common mortals they are. I introduce myself to both the younger ones, and have a pleasant conversation, although they appear slightly taken aback at my opening introduction.

'Hi, I'm Elizabeth. I used to be in The Way, but have attended another church for many years now.'

Nothing like breaking the ice with a sledgehammer. I know only too well that they commonly refer to other churches as being *of the devil*. I now discover that I spoke to one of the workers present twenty years ago, when I first left The Meetings. At that time, he and his older companion ridiculed my reading of a scriptural passage and called me the Anti-Christ. I decide to approach him, and re-introduce myself. The conversation does not go well. My tone becomes angry and my voice louder as he reveals himself to be a hardened, more savvy version of his younger self that I verbally jousted with decades previously. We quickly attract attention within the spacious but crowded lounge room, and it is known that I am causing trouble. My better judgement lapses under the grief of the circumstances and the rage I feel at my extended family still being held captive to this spiritual bondage.

The rage is sudden and unexpected. I have been an outsider for so long, far removed from all of this, with a fulfilled life and happy marriage. The death of my last grandparent now brings to the fore my spiritual separation from my wider family. I have broken the hearts of my grandparents and parents, and strained the boughs of my relationship with every other loved one in my family tree.

How did it come to this? More than twenty years ago I had committed my life to God, following the path of my ancestors to the fourth generation in *The True*

Way. Less than a year later, God presented me with a sharp turn in the path. I was about to be confronted by the God I professed to serve, and nothing would ever be the same again.

A Turn in the Path
February 1991

God was the hunter and I was the deer.
He stalked me... took unerring aim and fired.

- C S Lewis

There are certain turning points in life for which we have much anticipation and preparation. But the biggest ones often come about with breath-taking suddenness, altering our course and turning our lives upside down when least expected. At the time, we probably have no comprehension of the far-reaching effects of such moments. Such was the most significant turning point of my youth, the year I turned seventeen.

I was on the brink of my college education. In my hometown of Canberra, we gained our Higher School Certificate in this two-year period between high school and university. Although we complete our compulsory School Certificate at high school by the age of sixteen, college is still considered mandatory unless pursuing an apprenticeship in trade.

It was a brand new environment, but I knew many others from my former local high school. I entered my very first English class of the year and laid eyes on a stranger seated across the room.

What would you say if somebody told you that was the man you were going to marry one day?

It went through my mind exactly as if I had read it on a wall, a rudely confronting and unwelcome mental graffiti that shook me to the core. Inaudible, but shouted down the megaphone of my consciousness; phrased as a bizarre question rather than a prophetic statement. I stood frozen in the doorway, eyes unwillingly fixed on 'the man' undoubtedly in question, who was actually not much more than a boy, having barely turned sixteen. Ordinary to the point of plain, with brown hair and a thin, wiry adolescent frame, he sat slumped in a chair, alone in the corner of the classroom, with an air of slight dejection. Where had such a thought come from? My frozenness melted into an impulse to flee, and it now took all of my self-control not to turn and run from the room. What a ridiculous notion. Of course you're not going to marry him. Calm down. You would have to meet him, talk to him, and develop a relationship. All of which should be quite easy to avoid. I resolved at that point simply to have nothing to do with him.

Apart from a complete lack of attraction on my part, forming a relationship at school was out of the question. I was a *professing member* of The Way, God's only true church on earth. We didn't get involved with outsiders. Marrying an outsider would almost certainly result in severe censure of some form. Or - even worse - the questioning or loss of my own faith. I was fully committed to my faith in The True Way, and nothing was going to jeopardise that.

I was to find out the hard way that God had different plans. Plans to hunt me down, hound me unceasingly, and pull me out of this Way. I would prove to be a most unwilling and ungrateful participant of his sovereign plan for some time yet.

Born In Captivity
Childhood

...all effective propaganda must be confined to a few bare essentials and those must be expressed as far as possible in stereotyped formulas. These slogans should be persistently repeated until the very last individual has come to grasp the idea that has been put forward.

- 'War Propaganda', volume 1, chapter 6
of Mein Kampf (1925), by Adolf Hitler

I was born in 1974, in Canberra, Australia. My parents already belonged to this closed religious group that refused to give itself a name. In fact, I was fourth-generation one side and third-generation the other. We referred to our group as *The Way, The Truth, The Fellowship* or *The Meetings*, and called each other The Friends or *professing*. We refused a formal label, seeking to emphasize the point that we were not just another church, but the *One True Way*. We had our own persistently repeated slogans - *'The ministers without a home and the meetings in the home';* and *'The only church without a human founder'* among the best known.

It is very hard to define the doctrines of The Way, as we claimed to have no written creeds, doctrine or theology. The workers always said, 'our doctrine is in the Bible'. Most importantly, we did not have an earthly founder. No mere mortal had initiated our group, as had purportedly happened for every other Christian denomination and religious organisation on earth. No, we claimed exclusive and continuous origin from the apostles at the time of Christ himself. We took great pride in the fact that we were *not an organisation*, but just simple believers still following Jesus, *as it was in the beginning.* Our foundation was the ministry - workers sent out to preach in pairs just as Jesus first sent out his disciples (Matthew 10, Luke 10). The workers claimed this description as prescription, mandatory for all true ministers of Christ, for all time. Forsaking all earthly possessions and becoming homeless, somewhere along the way they also decided that workers should not marry.

Both men and women enter this ministry - expected to be for life - and preach in pairs in a locality for one year before being allocated to a different companion and location. A worker may stay in one place up to three years on the odd occasion, but their companion will usually change. Preaching partners are always of the same gender, and are usually comprised of one elder (more experienced) worker and one younger (newer) worker.

Like most cult adherents, I was strongly convinced that our way was the only 'right way' of salvation on earth. I did not, of course, identify myself as being in a cult. Such self-awareness in cult members is lacking, absorbed into the broader group mentality of special knowing and belonging. And yet every such group is essentially the same – having that special truth, that esoteric knowing that sets them apart from everyone else – the sure knowledge that they, and only they, own the gateway to God, and operate under the leadership of his only true agents on earth.

The inner world of the cult is a parallel world, an alternative reality, where we were aliens even within our own nation, race, culture and society. The first allegiance was not to God, family or friends, and submission was not firstly to the law. Above all else was submission to the leaders, and allegiance to the system, protecting its reputation at all costs. We knew we were different, not to be contaminated by those who were *worldly*. Worldly activities - entertainment, sports, groups, clubs and even friends – had to be eschewed or kept at arm's length. The worldly person was an inferior being who did not have the special knowledge and understanding of The True Way, causing us insiders to be cautious of revealing too much about what we knew and believed to the uninitiated. A worldly person could be brought into the system, of course, but it took a lot of careful handling and effort for them to be 'enlightened' enough to adopt the alien system as their own.

Within a cult exists a microcosm of a whole society, often with its own class system, ranging from royalty (related to the leaders) and superior (keeping all the rules), to middle class (good enough) and lower class (the misfits and rebels). At the very top is the leader, or leaders. In some cults this is a single person, originating with the founder, the mantle passed on from generation to generation to successive heads.

Within the Two-by-Twos, there are many leaders, known as *overseers* or *headworkers*, and there generally exists one for each major state within a country, or one for each smaller country. An overseer holds authority over all workers (members of the ministry) within his boundaries. The workers, in turn, hold authority over the non-ministry members, known as friends. The Two-by-Twos are cut sharply into this division of ministry and laity. All workers have authority over all friends, and if a worker should choose to exert this authority unjustly, there is little recourse available.

The fundamental nature of a cult is about authority reinforced by fear and control. The designated leaders wield extraordinary power over their underlings, who have no option but to respond in submission unless they want to risk being cast out into the world. To a people whose only sense of identity exists within the safety of the group, the thought of expulsion can be terrifying.

And yet a strange paradox exists. Most members will adamantly deny being either fearful or controlled. Conversely, many under this form of authoritarian leadership will express themselves as feeling safe and privileged. They feel safe from the evils *out there in the world* that they have been taught to fear, and privileged to have found God's chosen agents who will lead them in the right way. Those who are safely huddled in the nest of submission under the mother wings of *God's true servants* are likely to feel largely the warmth and comfort of mutual agreement. There they will be satisfied to remain, as long as they are content to live out their lives without questioning the status quo with too much rigour. As long as they are willing to relinquish responsibility for their spiritual welfare to those who know best, and feed only upon what they are given, life in the nest will seem like the only logical and safe place to be. They are permanent nest dwellers, held safely aloft from the world, their wings stunted and clipped into conformity, lest they ever learn to soar for themselves and gain autonomy from mother bird.

I was one of these safe and privileged people by birthright, a member of God's chosen, following the *one true ministry* as the only path to salvation. It was a life devoted to the workers, believing in and supporting their ministry, and going to the meetings.

Yet, despite being cosily ensconced in the nest of God's true people, the possibility of actually gaining salvation seemed as uncertain and fleeting as a shadow, its obtainability dependent upon one's standing at any one time in the prevailing conditions. There was a chance of salvation by virtue of being a professing member of The Way, but we still had to meet many conditions and live by many unwritten rules. The conditions and rules could change at any time, dependent upon the strictness of the workers on rotation in the locality in any given year. Most importantly, we had to strive to *meet the standard*, personified in the character of Jesus.

As a child, I heard repeatedly that Jesus was perfect, and that we had to seek to follow his example. He *lived to show us how to live*, and we had to exert every effort to try to be as good as he was, in order to be good enough for salvation. This puzzled me greatly. What exactly constituted this 'perfection'? Jesus always did the right thing, obviously, but did he ever get sick or hurt? I couldn't imagine a perfect person with a hacking cough or a stubbed toe. Did he ever have morning hair, or was it always perfect too, never a hair out of place? Something did not make sense. Being perfect was an exceptionally tall order, and I did not need anyone to tell me I would never measure up. In general, I was a responsible and diligent child who rarely got into trouble, but I knew that I was far from perfect. I had enough logical capacity to grasp - even as a small child - that it was impossible to be perfect for even half a day, no matter how hard I tried.

My two younger brothers and I went to the local public school. Despite *worldly influences*, the Two-by-Twos generally send their children to public schools. Workers frown on Christian schools, stating that other Christians teach *false doctrines of men*. They consider it far worse to be exposed to the influence of other Christians than almost all forms of secular teaching.

Perhaps because we were not permitted to have a television set, I was an avid reader from a young age. My primary school library permitted the borrowing of only one book at a time, which had to be returned before another could be loaned. I borrowed a book every day, and was eventually given special dispensation to borrow three books on a Friday so I would have enough to read over the weekend. One book particularly stands out in my memory from childhood. Robin Klein's *People Might Hear You* told the story of a young girl who suddenly finds herself part of a fanatical sect when her guardian aunt marries. I identified strongly with the protagonist, Frances, who tried hard to be a 'worthy member of the temple' but was often failing to live up to the standard and was afraid to voice her many private doubts. She, however, was home schooled and never allowed to leave the house. She was not even permitted to make a noise loud enough for the neighbours to hear ('people might hear you'). To outsiders, she simply did not exist at all.

I could clearly see how Frances became conditioned to her new circumstances and developed irrational fears as a result. But it seemed completely different from my situation. Frances had been deceived by a cult. I *knew* that everything I believed in was true. Despite this, it was a disquieting exposure to the realisation that there might be other groups in the world who also believed they were the *only right way*. How could I be sure that *my* way was right?

The main difference I discerned between myself and classmates was that my family did not have a television and were not supposed to listen to the radio or other

recorded music. This was the era of ET and Star Wars -
my primary school years - and I frequently relied on
others to bring me up to speed on contemporary
culture, as I was hopelessly uninformed. Consider, if
you will, a 10 year old girl trying to explain the plot of
Star Wars to another 10 year old girl who hasn't seen it.
Ewoks were, from what I could gather, something like
teddy bears with weapons. What this had to do with
spaceships was hard to fathom. No one could
understand why I had no television at home, and I did
not know either. I ran around the playground with the
rest of the children shouting 'ET phone home', not
having a clue who ET was or why he was always
wanting to phone home.

I was obsessed with ballet during my primary
school years. While my friends were preoccupied with
horses or rock stars, I was trying to stand *en pointe*.
Undertaking a worldly activity like ballet was not
considered suitable for The Friends. Mum thought it
could be useful training for posture and deportment (I
slouched terribly), but Dad could not bring himself to
agree to such an endeavour, knowing the workers
would disapprove. When all Mum's efforts to enrol me
in a ballet class were thwarted, she bought me a pink
leotard as consolation. She took me down to the nearby
community hall to see the local ballet class, where I
watched with envy across the broad expanse of worn
floorboards as they warmed up at the barre. They
might as well have been across the broad expanse of
the Pacific Ocean. I was beginning to understand that
my parents did not hold the ultimate authority in my
life. Somehow these people called workers did.
Somehow, they behaved like parents to all of us, telling
us where we could go and what we could do. We

seemed to be part of a separate system from other people. A system in which we were excluded from the activities of ordinary people.

Not participating in any worldly activities included any kind of sports. We could not join a Saturday morning sports team or watch a local game. If school friends wanted to know why, I had no answers; it was not ours to question why. In sports lessons at school I was a fish out of water. I had extremely poor hand-eye coordination and could not catch or kick a ball. Doing sports at school could be excruciating. Not permitted to wear trousers as a Two-by-Two female, it was extremely embarrassing to be the only one wearing a skirt for Physical Education. It definitely was not the modest option on the sporting field. My mother was more practical and did concede this point as I got older, permitting me to wear track pants for sports.

Growing up in Australia, where football and rugby league are the two main national 'religions', exclusion from all forms of sport resulted in further separation from my own nation's culture. Much to the amusement of my friends, I still do not understand the difference between the two codes. Cricket, also, remains an enigma.

The only acceptable extra-curricular activity for The Friends was music lessons, preferably the piano. My two younger brothers and I dutifully took piano lessons for most of our childhood. It took me a long time to figure out the purpose of this - we might one day be able to play accompaniment for hymns in a *gospel meeting*, the public services held weekly by workers.

Not being able to do ballet was certainly the greatest disappointment of my childhood, especially as nobody could tell me why. Nevertheless, we had a lot to make up for it. My brothers and I had an enviable comic book collection and spent countless hours engrossed in The Phantom, Archie, Footrot Flats, Asterix and Tintin. We had a large collection of board games that we played fairly regularly. I taught my brother how to play chess from the instruction booklet in a chess set we found. Mostly I read - voraciously.

Keeping the Standard

We have often said in our meetings that there are two things fundamental to the faith of Jesus: the homelessness of the preacher and the church in the home and only in the home. Whenever we depart from these two fundamentals we have departed from the faith, we have become apostate. We must contend to the very end of the chapter for the homelessness of the preacher and the church in the home and only in the home.

- Jack Carroll, Hayden Lake sermon 1932,
www.tellingthetruth.info

One of the great difficulties of a childhood in a cult is questions from outsiders. What is your church? What is its name? Where do you meet? What do you believe? If these questions are fundamentally difficult for the average cult member, they are amplified for the Two-by-Twos. We did not have a name. We did not have a building. I was not even sure what we believed. Our responses sounded untruthful, evasive. The typical answers we were forced to give outsiders were met with great scepticism. My reply usually started with 'It's kind of hard to explain…'

Workers and parents sometimes suggested telling outsiders that we were a *non-denominational Christian church*. I could not fathom what this was supposed to mean. What was a denomination? Weren't Christians *of the devil*? Churches had *false doctrines*. To me, that answer made the least sense. We children concealed our faith in any way possible in order to avoid such questions, and carried this habit into adulthood. I have observed that the average adult Two-by-Two still seeks to conceal his faith and avoid questions wherever possible. Most neighbours and work peers would have no idea about the beliefs or practices of The Way, even upon enquiry. While the outward appearance of the women tends to be a billboard advertisement of adherence to something, the company name and contact details are strangely absent, exuding palpable secrecy. When questions are met with a strange reluctance, people learn not to ask the questions. Yes, this is how the group that believes it is the 'only true way' carries out its evangelism – with silence and non-disclosure.

One of the foremost issues for females in The Way is hair, which must be long and preferably uncut. Mine was a constant hassle in my younger years. Being quite fine, it tangled often and severely. One small knot could quickly take hold and multiply, creating a rat's nest. Keeping it knot free was a painful business and constant headache, literally. I sometimes longed for a change, to have my hair cut just a bit shorter, but Dad hated me having my hair cut at all, and nothing more than a trim of the very ends was acceptable.

When I was about nine years old, I did succeed, quite sneakily, in getting my hair cut almost to shoulder length. It had grown exceptionally long, almost to my waist, and it was finally agreed, after much pleading but still against the noted objection of my father, that I could have a number of inches taken off. Haircuts were always done at home, and Mum wasn't sure of the best approach to cutting off so much at once. Eventually she braided it, and cut the braid off at what seemed a reasonable length, in the middle of my back. Once released from the braid, it needed some re-cutting to even things up. I kept tilting my head slightly to one side then the other as Mum attempted to re-cut it into a straight line. She just could not get my hair even. It got shorter and shorter the more she tried. It eventually ended up at shoulder length, and Dad was not happy. I was thrilled, but I certainly had the shortest hair of anyone at The Meetings. Having my hair cut did not seem like a big deal; I could not understand the fuss. It was not for some years that I discovered that some of my female peers had never had their hair cut. Some of them did eventually decide – in their teens - that modest trims to remove split ends might be acceptable. This seemed more preferable than burning the ends as they had heard some girls did (so as to be able to say they had never 'cut' their hair, beneficial in terms of pure legalism only).

Once a *professing* member, there was a strong expectation that women had to wear their hair in a bun. The requirement to have the longest hair possible, only to pin it into the shortest hairstyle possible, was obviously a deeply spiritual matter far beyond the logic of yours truly. We simply understood that buns were a sign of God's true people. An older professing woman once told me a story about spotting a group of women at a market overseas. She just *knew by the spirit* that they belonged to The Way. The spirit, she emphasized, was the same the world over, and The Friends could recognise it in each other, even as strangers (this is a very common belief among the Two-by-Twos). I suggested it probably had far more to do with the fact that they all had the same hairdo. She became quite angry when I would not accept that such recognition was *by the spirit*.

I observed from a young age that women in The Way had a different appearance to those *in the world*. We were not to perm or colour our hair. I did not know anyone who went to a hairdresser. It is now hard to believe that I continued to cut my own hair for many years after I left, until I had an epiphany one day that it was not wrong to go to a salon.

Makeup and jewellery were also evil, and females were not to wear trousers of any kind. As a result, I quickly learned to judge everyone's depth of faith and chance of salvation by their outward appearance. Newcomers to The Way were assured there were no such 'rules'. Albeit denied publicly, these conditions of membership were very real and well known to those within the movement. New converts were eased in gradually under the guise of *obedience to the spirit*. No one would tell them what to do during the honeymoon period, but they would eventually have to prove they had *the right spirit*. This meant cottoning on to the fact that they needed to change their appearance to look more like everyone else. Conformity was the greatest sign of unity. If the spirit proved a little tardy in providing instruction, a worker would be sure to help them along.

One continuing problem though, was that the code of dress could fluctuate from town to town. It could also depend purely on the whim of a particular worker. A peer of mine was commanded to grow her fringe (bangs) out before she was baptized. Some of her baptized friends had similar hairstyles, but this was irrelevant. Her submission to God would not be evident unless she obeyed this particular command from the worker who was baptizing her.

Clothing for attending group meetings was very formal. Men wore a shirt and tie with suit trousers, while women wore conservative mid-calf dresses or sleeved blouses and long skirts. I lived in a small city, where standards were more liberal than those of our rural counterparts. In country circles, a host of other considerations were necessary. Forbidden apparel may include sleeves shorter than a certain length, open-toed shoes, heels that were too high, coloured shoes, and decorative watches that looked too much like jewellery. Dresses had to be long, but could not be too long. More than a hymn book length from the ground was just extra fabric for sheer vanity (and could be too flattering). Mid-calf was the preference, as modelled by the female workers. I learned these important additional rules while attending the annual conventions, and from friends who were apparently far more attuned to our culture than I was.

My father was brought up in the State of Victoria under strict Two-by-Two observances in a very conservative family. My mother was accustomed to far more leniency, especially when it came to hair and dress. To my father, hair in a bun was mandatory for all professing women attending a meeting. My mother thought nothing of wearing her hair down, and struggled to conform to my father's expectations. She permitted me to wear track pants and jeans at home and for some casual outings. This was unheard of for most other girls my age with whom I went to meetings. It also remained a source of friction between my parents. We lived in a climate with very cold winters, and my mother preferred I keep warm in tracksuits on a winter's day for playing rather than having to wear a skirt and stockings. I was somewhat bemused by the seriousness with which the rules were upheld by others, and must confess I failed to take them very seriously myself.

One day I returned home from an outing with a neighbourhood friend and recognised the car in our driveway as one regularly used by the workers. I went into a panic - I could not walk into the house and greet the workers while wearing jeans. It would also be a great embarrassment to my father. My outsider friend must have gone home to her parents with an interesting story that day. I had to sneak around the back of my own house and try to get in and up to my bedroom without being seen, just because I was wearing jeans.

Yes, I was becoming a religious hypocrite. Cults beget rules, rules beget rule-breakers, rule-breakers start to beget hypocrisy and secrets. The majority of rules I 'broke' pertained to ridiculously small things such as the unwritten dress code or hair length. But once we were called on as a family to keep a bigger secret. The year was 1986, and Crocodile Dundee had hit the cinemas. There was nary a soul in the entire country - perhaps even the entire western world – who hadn't seen this film (apart from The Friends). It is not exaggerating to say that it was the talk of the nation. My two younger brothers and I were astounded to be informed by our parents that we would go to the cinema to see it as a family. We knew that this would be a big secret. There could be no slip-ups. No accidental mention of it to anyone at The Meetings. This was to be, literally, a once-in-a-lifetime event. We promised to keep it a family matter and off we went, our earnestness in wanting to keep this promise sincere. We ultimately failed, as the topic inevitably arose, and we did not tell lies. It was the number one rule in our family – no matter what we did, lying about it was far worse. Mum ended up cheerfully admitting to some of The Friends that we had been to see it.

The alternative was to try to keep all of the unwritten rules, all the time. This required a form of spiritual gymnastics, as the ever-changing standards also varied from worker to worker. I know people who grew up in those strict households. For many, the standard was so high that failure was a relentless companion. Parents constantly tried to exact the perfect behaviour and conformity from their children, sometimes causing them to be unreasonably harsh and uncompromising. Children had a miserable time at school because they were the weird ones, excluded from certain activities with no reasonable explanation. Daughters were forced to wear skirts for sports and hiking, or not participate. Most social activities or events with school friends were out of the question. For many, a childhood in The Way was miserable; the exclusions nonsensical and the standard of perfection unobtainable. It is little wonder that a significant number have given up on any form of faith altogether after coming of age.

The long list of unwritten rules became more and more oppressive as we reached our teens. The workers maintained admirable control – and continuity in The Way – through conditioning and fear. If I left The Way, there was a good chance that everyone would be standing around my grave a week later. We heard stories of this nature often, especially at convention. The consequences likely to befall those who were unfaithful to The Way were more than inferred. There was usually the accompanying example of some nameless unfortunate soul who had met such a fate.

Going to the Meeting

My hope of salvation is the blood of Christ. But I would like to explain to you what it means. The blood of Christ is the ministry and the church in the home. Without the New Testament ministry you don't have the blood of Christ which includes the church in the home. The forgiveness of sins is a fringe benefit.

- Leo Stancliffe, worker, 1981, www.workersect.org

While my childhood saw a general adherence to most of the main rules, I learned more of the culture from peers rather than my parents. Spending time with many of The Friends in The Way while growing up, many more rules about the way things were done came to my attention. And, of course, many hours were spent every week at meetings, being further habituated. There were Sunday morning, Sunday night and Wednesday night meetings held in someone's home. Then there were *gospel meetings*, held two nights a week from March – October each year in Australia, outside of the summer *convention* period. *Gospel meetings* - or *The Mission* as it was also known - was held on a Sunday evening (in lieu of the Sunday night home meeting) and one other mid-week night. We met in a rented community hall or school gymnasium / auditorium. Workers expected everyone within a 100km radius to attend these public meetings. If we were lucky, the mid-week gospel meeting would be held on a Wednesday night, replacing the Wednesday night home meeting. More often than not, though, another night was chosen - often a Tuesday, Thursday or Friday night. This meant we still had to attend Wednesday night home meetings, totalling four meetings a week. Apart from the sheer number of meetings to attend, they moved location every year, and sometimes several times in a year. Sometimes they were held out of town, an hour or more away. All meetings were compulsory, and no one could conceive of simply electing not to attend. There were years when we spent more than ten hours every week travelling to and from and attending meetings. It was not unusual to return home at 9 or 10pm on a week night after a regular meeting, even as young children.

Meeting attendance was drilled into members with the rigour of military training. Stories about the lengths to which Two-by-Twos would go to be faithful in their meeting attendance were legendary. I recall whole sermons containing nothing more than example after example of how much faithful effort some members expended in getting to the meetings. These stories were told in a similar vein to the grand old tradition of how hard it was for grandfather to get to school in his day (knee deep in snow with no shoes, etc.). I know of such instances within my own extended family. A relative recounts a day in her childhood when the family was ready for the meeting, but the car would not start. A repairman was called, and after much waiting and tinkering, the vehicle was finally running – almost an hour later. Nevertheless, they still set off for the meeting, arriving for the last five minutes of the service. Such determination at least showed others that they had not meant to miss the meeting, and in fact would go to any lengths to attend, even if only for the last few minutes.

Other stories are far more sobering and heartbreaking. Another relative recounts a well-known story from his grandfather's generation. A younger son in the family was complaining of severe stomach pain, but it was meeting time. The family, including the young son, piled into the car and headed off for the meeting. On arrival, this boy was in such a bad state that he could not go in. He was left in the car alone while the rest of his family attended. More than an hour later they came back to find him dead – his appendix had burst.

It takes stories like this to appreciate the heights to which meetings are elevated - it is the meetings themselves that are worshipped, rather than the God of the Bible in whose name they meet.

The gospel meetings themselves were mind-numbing. Week after week, several times a week, we sat in yet another community hall or school gymnasium, gazing at the basketball line markings on the scuffed linoleum floor or counting stripes on the shirt of someone seated in the forward row. For much of my childhood I developed a zoning-out mechanism, planning in advance what topic to daydream about in the next gospel meeting. The preaching was conducive to a dulling of the mind and enhancement of emotional attachment, a never-ending refrain about the importance of *the ministers without a home and the meetings in the home*. Workers often developed their own sing-song rhythmic rising and falling of tone and pitch - a constant lullaby keeping listeners appeased and contented in the arms of the ministry, spiritual infants who lacked understanding but cleaved to the comfort and boundaries of their spiritual family, no matter how odd or dysfunctional.

The congregational singing was mournful, joyless. The pondering slowness - unbearable to outsiders - supposedly engendered reverence. Anything too upbeat or joyful was considered an affront to true holiness, which is apparently solemn and expressionless. Some members delighted in developing their own signature style, complementing the proceedings with zealous but harsh guttural wailings.

Despite their efforts at evangelism through gospel meetings held in public buildings, the fundamental cornerstone of the Two-by-Twos is the *meeting in the home*. Considered a foundational principle of the New Testament church, the teaching of meeting in a home for fellowship has been elevated to the status of their second most important doctrine (the first being a Two-by-Two homeless ministry). Of course, it is the common practice of most mainstream Christian churches to have smaller weekly Bible studies in private homes, alongside their larger corporate worship services, but in the realm of Two-by-Twoism, this apparently doesn't count; Two-by-Twos see only themselves as attaining the true spirit of meeting and worshipping in a home.

In home meetings, where all professing members have a turn at praying and speaking for several minutes each, I spent a lot of time in mental calculation. If there were fifteen people to speak, and each person spoke on average for so many minutes, I could calculate fairly accurately when the meeting would end. For the sheer mental engagement, I also quickly recalculated after the end of each testimony; a prisoner of the meeting marking time on the wall of my mind.

Sometimes there is a flexing of worker authority muscles by sending members to a different home meeting than their preferred choice, simply to test (or enforce) obedience. They dictate which home meeting members will attend, and members generally go where they are told without dispute, even if it means having to travel much further than the nearest meeting. It was often a great disappointment to learn that your family had been assigned to a different meeting, and that you would therefore be separated from your friends. Such decisions were often made for practical reasons, but it also appeared to be the workers' intent to separate particular friendships that they deemed too close or too loyal.

While I was in high school, there was a major change. The meeting was to come to our house. This elevated my father to the position of elder, facilitating the meetings in our home. Saturday nights took on the ritual of vacuuming, cleaning and setting up the meeting room, a task that fell primarily to me.

Our meetings, rituals and physical appearance rendered us a peculiar people. Whatever the cultural oddities, these were my people, my fellow aliens. There was no doubt that I was very firmly embedded in The Way, born in captivity and conditioned to all the nuances that made up our small world within the Two-by-Twos. I knew of no relatives outside The Meetings. My grandparents, aunts, uncles and cousins - on both sides - were all in. My father was one of nine siblings and my mother one of seven. With all of their siblings married and most with children, I had many relatives in The Way. Even my closest friends - who were not blood relatives - had cousins in common with me. Many of my relations were farmers and landowners.

Although I grew up in the city, I spent many of my school holidays on farms, particularly with my maternal grandparents. I attended their home meetings and gospel meetings, developing further friendships within the group. Nana and Papa were kind and generous to me. Alongside their loyalty to the workers, their love for God was evident. Nana taught me to memorise Psalm 23 (*The Lord is My Shepherd*) from an early age. They held their own lengthy morning devotions every day - studying the Bible, reading books about scripture and praying. Despite their deep disappointment when I left The Meetings and married an outsider, they continued to welcome us both into their home. Papa was a remarkable man, despite being the offspring of a difficult marriage; his father had a reputation for harshness and cruelty. Becoming the protector of his siblings from a young age, he later also became a provider for his mother and youngest sibling. He delayed his own marriage for years to finish putting his brother through school. When he was finally able to marry, he and Nana continued to provide a home for his mother who had been through a nasty and very public divorce. In those days, such an occurrence was rare. My great-grandmother had first attended Two-by-Two meetings as a young married woman, bringing her children along with her. My great-grandfather did not attend The Meetings.

The Work of the Workers

How many of us are really clear on the conditions that must be fulfilled by those who are to have a part in this ministry? God's people demand greater sacrifices from their preachers than any other people in the world. They insist that the preachers must sacrifice all, and they say they believe in no other kind of preachers but those who sacrifice all for the Gospel's sake.

- Jack Carroll, early worker, www.tellingthetruth.info

The styling of the ministry of the workers is the first and most important foundational doctrine of The Way, the external container into which every other belief is fitted.

The workers claim to *live by faith*. When they *enter the work*, they are required to give away or sell their earthly possessions. Any personal funds are then usually handed over to the ministry in a show of undivided commitment. Being homeless by design, they live at the homes of lay members, The Friends. They base themselves in one location for most of the year, but move around visiting the homes of members in the locality, staying a night or two at a time. It is also common for them to come for dinner with each family for *a visit* at least once during the year or two in which they remain in a particular *field* (town or region). Such overnight stays and short visits are mandated and set by the workers, who usually invite themselves and set the respective date. Such an arrangement was not refused unless extreme circumstances prevailed, no matter how inconvenient. It was considered a great privilege that a worker would deign to visit your home, an occasion calling for the best china, cutlery, menu and of course, behaviour. While these visits could be nerve-wracking in wanting to measure up to the standard under the scrutiny of our spiritual authorities, they were also generally positive.

That said, the worst punishment I ever received as a child came about by having a worker over for dinner. That night I was playing checkers (drafts) with my younger brother. The visiting worker sided with my brother and started making his moves on the board for him. My brother - a regular opponent in board games - was suddenly gaining an unfair advantage. I considered this cheating and told the worker so. The next day I received a severe punishment for speaking out against something a worker had done. I was outraged at the injustice of it. I had not misbehaved or done anything disobedient; I had merely been objecting to unfair play. This was probably a childish and immature response, but hardly worthy of severe punishment. Workers, apparently, were always right, no matter the context. The lesson seemed to be that I was to accept without question anything they chose to do.

Workers had very little to do with their time, and were often keen to do odd jobs around the house rather than spend endless hours sitting, eating and talking. Hosts tended to refuse such offers, however, wanting to treat God's servants as visiting royalty. This must have resulted in severe boredom much of the time for many workers.

While a worker or two stayed with us very occasionally, our house was not suited to regular or long-term stays. Workers preferred their own private quarters and bathrooms where possible, something we could not offer. Years later, I discovered that I was far more fortunate than some, who as children became the victims of sexual assaults within their own homes by these visiting members of the ministry. While these instances were not common, subsequent accounts have shown that if an offending worker was reported to a head worker, the perpetrator was simply moved to another town, state or even country. Victims and their families who made a fuss about the assaults and went to the police, report being vilified by other members for bringing The Way into disrepute. I have heard of at least one account where families were expressly forbidden by their overseer to testify in court against the offender. That particular offender did go on to be successfully prosecuted and found guilty of serious offences against one victim, but never spent a day in jail. The judge was unaware at the time of many more victims known to police who could not be compelled to testify.[1]

[1] Australian senior worker Ernie Barry, convicted 19 May 2011, Latrobe Valley Magistrates', Victoria, Australia.

'Coming Apart to Rest'

We are God's chosen people. Our main objectives are to serve the workers, attend gospel meetings and conventions and honour The Truth.

- Los Angeles Special Meeting, March 10, 1985, www.workersect.org

Conventions were the annual highlight of the calendar - a four-day spiritual retreat camp for members, each convention catering for several hundred attendees. Situated on privately owned properties across the country, these gatherings were staggered by date and geography across the Australian summer. Scores of identical white canvas tents were set up in rows in bare dusty paddocks, strapped to interlocking wooden poles with thick ropes. Men's and women's areas were divided, each with its own toilet and shower block. These were still primitive in the extreme when I last attended a convention in New South Wales in the early 1990s. The Way mocks any form of organisation, and does not believe in church buildings. Therefore, nothing can appear too customised, and should instead have every appearance of a temporary camp in the wilderness, rather like the Israelites in the desert. This included - in my day - pit toilets and cold showers. Modern day requirements of environmental impact considerations and health and safety standards are now starting to catch up with these former arrangements. Significant money has been poured into modernising facilities in the past decade or so. Hopefully this will address the lack of expertise or training in food handling, which, coupled with inadequate storage facilities at many of these conventions, has been known to cause outbreaks of diarrhoea and food poisoning.

The worst episode I ever heard about in this regard concerned a number of workers who contracted salmonella during convention preparations in Oregon USA, in 1989, recounted to me by former American worker Brad Lewis.[2] Despite his and a number of fellow workers being desperately ill, they were told not to go to a doctor. Suffering severe vomiting and diarrhoea, some were housed in trailers [caravans] with no restroom facilities, around 150 metres from the nearest toilet block. It was Brad's first year out in the work, and he had just sold all his possessions and given them to the headworker as requested. He had no health insurance, and no way of seeking medical assistance for himself, either physically or financially. When he no longer had the strength to make it to the toilet block, he was forced to relieve himself in the bushes nearest his trailer.

When convention attendees arrived some days later and meetings commenced, Brad and his fellow workers were still desperately ill, and now dehydrated from days of vomiting and diarrhoea. The totality of care provided was being 'checked on' twice a day and provided with saltine crackers. As Brad lay shivering with fever and listening to the sounds of convention obliviously carrying on around him, he began to wonder if 'giving my life for the work' was to be far more literal than he'd thought. His older companion seemed passively resigned to the fact that he might die, even suggesting as much.

No one had told Brad's family of his illness and condition, so when Brad's mother arrived at convention she wondered where he was. She finally insisted on seeing him. Finding him shaking and feverish and discovering he had been in this state for some days, she knew he needed an ambulance and medical attention. Her request was finally permitted by the workers with a caveat that no ambulance siren could be used near or on the convention grounds. When examined and questioned by the attending paramedics, Brad could not even name the American President. He passed out on the way to hospital and woke up a day later not knowing where he was. Medical treatment was also finally sought for two female workers who were severely dehydrated. A potential tragedy was only narrowly averted.

Why did seeking medical treatment for seriously ill companions apparently not enter into the equation for the organising senior workers of this convention? In a group known for its secrecy, they would have been particularly loath to allow the prying eyes of outsiders onto convention grounds. It also appears they did not want to risk inspectors shutting down their operation days before attendees arrived. Even if the source of the salmonella was not identified and many more were in danger of becoming ill, the show must go on, even if people died for the cause.

Willing helpers attend *preps* (preparations) in the days and weeks before each convention to erect the wooden poles and canvas tents. Thousands of items are pulled out of storage, right down to tea kettles, china plates and salt and pepper shakers. Tables and benches are set up in a large barn-like structure for meals, and a huge shed or tent serves as the meeting place. Friends may nominate which convention they would like to attend, but approval must still be granted by a worker. Some locations are certainly more favourable than others. In places, summer temperatures can reach 40 degrees Celsius (104 degrees Fahrenheit), from which there is no respite. Certain conventions were also considered to have a 'more superior standard of saint, as it were' (as phrased by a Canberra contemporary of ours). I guess he preferred to avoid particular conventions reputed to be frequented by more 'lowly' rural folk.

As children, convention was much anticipated, perhaps because it was a bit of a camping adventure. We met up with old friends from across the state and made many new ones. These friends understood this common tribe to which we all belonged, without the difficult explanations that so often accompanied friendships with outsiders.

From the time we entered the convention grounds at the gate each year (guarded by workers), we really did enter a different world, an alternative reality far removed from normal life. There was a strong expectation that everyone would remain on site continuously for the four full days in order to be completely *separate from the world* without the spell being broken. In this monastic environment, time between meetings and meals was reserved for assigned chores, quiet talking together, Bible reading or napping as the only approved pursuits. From the cocoon of convention we stepped blinkingly back into the strong noises and bright glare of the world as though wakened from a strange dream.

Convention was a tightly ordered environment that ran to an exact schedule of mealtimes, meeting times and quiet times from sun up to sun down. No games, no sports, no recreation. Workers patrolled the commons around the meeting and meal sheds at the close of each day, brandishing torches that they shone into dark corners and up trees. They cleared the grounds of all individuals, especially courting couples. Did anyone ever really hide up a tree in an attempt to evade the late evening rounds of a worker, or was it simply deterrence? These shepherds exerted all due diligence to ensure that every last sheep was safely corralled into their gender division before lights were extinguished for the night.

You may imagine that clothing would be more casual at a convention held in sheds and tents on a farming property in the Australian mid-summer heat, but this was definitely not the case. Dress remained very formal, convention wardrobes planned for weeks beforehand. New dresses for convention were highly desired, especially for young single females of marriageable age. Women and we teenage girls tramped around these farms in the dust, flies and heat of an Australian summer in our stiletto heels, stockings and pretty frocks (this training has afforded me the dubious talent of being able to run in high heels on almost any terrain). The men and boys dutifully trudged about in their dress trousers, shirts and ties. All dreaded the last day of convention when four days' culmination of human waste and heat in the long trench under the pit toilet blocks would climax in an unbearable assault on the senses.

When it came to personal grooming, the austere amenities afforded little in the way of assistance in regards to mirrors and shelves needed for wrestling hair in pouffed buns, French plaits and French rolls. Hundreds of women struggled each day in their tents with brushes, hairspray and dozens of bobby pins to create their regular and often elaborate hairdos. A pouffed bun is a tricky thing to accomplish well, often necessitating five or six attempts to get it just right. Many women wrapped their hair around false hairpieces. Sometimes these were created from their own moultings, rolled and compressed into shape. While power sockets were very rare in the women's amenities, the men fared a little better, as they were all required to shave every day. Moustaches and beards, although common in earlier days of the group, were now considered inappropriate.

Over the four days of convention, there were three meetings every day. Two hours in the morning, two hours after lunch (in which many struggled to stay awake) and at least one more hour after dinner. Several hundred attendees would quietly file into the huge metal barn at least 15 minutes before each service and sit in complete silence until it began. Concertina fans were unfurled and furiously flapped back and forth. Seats at the very back of the barn were highly coveted, where one might catch a slight breeze from the open back doors to provide relief against the stifling heat of the interior. Seating was on primitive wooden benches, with cushions brought from home to ease the hardness of four days of almost continuous sitting. This, combined with a definite lack of incentive to pay a visit to the pit toilet block, resulted in lots of convention constipation (unless, of course, there was a diarrhoea outbreak). The only respite from the relentless heat was the rare year we had rainfall, providing great relief in temperature but a number of additional challenges. Dusty bare ground metamorphosed into a minefield of puddles and mud, all to be negotiated in heels or dress shoes. Heavier rains thundered on the tin roof of the meeting shed, making anything except perpetual hymn singing impossible.

Workers always sat separately, in reserved rows at the front of the meeting shed, side-on to the speaker's platform. From there, they could observe all attendees during meetings. The only time out from hearing worker after worker speak was the *time of testimonies*. This occurred in at least one meeting each day, an opportunity for professing members to stand and address the entire meeting. When the time was announced, those wishing to give a testimony would stand and wait their turn. Testimonies were a welcome diversion, but most the same in their essence:

'I've really struggled this past year, and had so many times of failure, and sometimes I didn't think I was going to make it, but it is so good to be back here again at convention, among God's people, and it means that I've made it through another year. I just want to strive to continue in The Way and to be more worthy and do better in the coming year.'

We saw conventions as the pit stop, a fresh start. We resolved to do better, try harder, and genuinely be more worthy in the year to come. Conventions were themed along the lines of *coming apart from the world to rest*, and *to be refreshed* for the next lap of being *out there in the world*.

We ate meals in a large shed where very basic wooden tables and benches were arranged in continuous rows to accommodate the large number of attendees. Meals were usually served in two sittings, both to cater for numbers, and so that some could serve while others ate (and vice versa). Most attendees were assigned jobs. These ranged from refilling condiment containers and setting tables, through to peeling vegetables, cooking, washing up or being a waiter. Jobs tended to be associated with status. I did not belong to a family of superior saints, nor was I closely related to any workers. I was finally deemed worthy enough, one year, of the humble job of refilling the sugar bowls.

The desire of every teenage boy was to get the most coveted job of being a *tea boy*. Gripping a very large kettle, these boys would patrol the aisles of the meal shed, shouting 'whi-i-te tea! whi-i-te tea!' in the wail of a street seller against his competitor who cried 'bla-a-ck tea!'. Those wanting the tea of choice would quickly present their cup to the aisle behind them as the tea boy passed by. As it was the only possibility of getting a hot caffeine beverage at convention, the tea boys were exceptionally well loved by the attendees who waited impatiently for these choruses to begin.

The workers had special tables reserved for them at one end of the meal shed, and did not sit with the general folk. Actually, they had special everything, from tableware and cutlery to a varied menu. The rest of us had to supply our own cutlery, carried about in a custom-made fabric bag or pencil case. Occasionally some poor unsuspecting soul would accidentally sit at a worker table, only to be quickly shooed off by the waiter. Being headwaiter of the worker table was, needless to say, the ultimate privilege, reserved only for the most faithful of male saints.

It is only fair to mention that some workers hated this system of separation and tried to sit with the common folk. Such episodes did not end well. Other workers saw it as trying to increase popularity with the flock, and making the rest of them look bad. Issues of jealousy were rife among the workers over which of them were more popular with The Friends. Any worker not keeping to their separated status was quickly chastened and forced back onto their pedestal. Older workers believed it did nothing for the reputation of the ministry to have its adherents lowered to the status of common mortals.

If I miss anything about convention, it is the food. It was very simple fare, and the menu was the same every day - year in, year out - but I absolutely loved the porridge, cooked from rough ground wheat. I also quite liked the lunchtime stew. My husband, who believes he would rather starve than eat porridge, and has no love of stew, has declared that convention must be a terrible place indeed, if porridge and stew are highlights.

---

[2] Memoirs of former worker Brad Lewis and personal correspondence with the author (Boring Convention Grounds 1989, Oregon, USA). Included with consultation and permission.

Adolescence

What would be appropriate apparel for girls to wear skiing, horseback riding, jogging, etc.? Some things are pretty hard to do and be a Christian, and if you don't deny yourself anything, it is pretty hard to fulfil scripture. "If any man will come after me let him deny himself, and take up his cross, and follow me.'

- Eldon Tenniswood, US Worker,
Young People's Meetings, California 1982

When reminiscing on the past, it is very easy to remember only the good or only the bad, and paint a picture according to one's preference. Despite the events that have unfolded since, overall I have good memories of my childhood. I had parents who loved me and praised my accomplishments. I was well provided for in a stable home at a time when friends at school increasingly had parents who were getting divorced. We had a large menagerie of pets, and spent most of our school holidays down at the coast, usually playing on the beach or fishing from our small boat, which we would use to explore the estuaries on the south coast of New South Wales. When not camping, we would rent a holiday house, complete with a television set, and get up early every morning to watch the cartoons (watching TV was not a sin, just owning one!).

Life as one of The Friends was also generally good, with a strong sense of camaraderie. We had occasional get-togethers for a night of hymn singing or a potluck dinner, especially during the years we had workers assigned to us who allowed socialising outside of meetings. Let me just say, sometimes the 'pot luck' bit was literal. Everyone would bring a selection of tinned food to place into the very large cooking pot, and we would eat the resulting stew for dinner. Of course, someone would find it extremely funny to bring some empty dog food cans and discreetly place them among the other empty cans, which could be viewed once we had eaten. Humour, Two-by-Two style.

The formation of my own identity was beginning to consolidate as I moved from childhood years into early adolescence. For me, the age of fourteen was when I began, consciously, to make my own decisions leading towards maturity and independence. Identified by primary school teachers as a more forceful personality who was a leader rather than a follower, I commenced high school running with a more 'in' crowd. Within two years my grades had dropped, and I felt more and more at odds with myself in that friendship group. By the age of fourteen I made a conscious decision to change friends and change direction. I was the rare person who exited one of these more exclusive friendship groups voluntarily; those with influence usually kicked unwanted ones out in unpleasant circumstances. Even more unusually, there were no ill feelings, and I maintained a good relationship with those I left behind.

Some other events soon tested my mettle and further shaped the development of my character. One of my younger brothers commenced high school about this time, and came to the attention of some bullies. Whenever they spotted me, they would target me as his sister, yelling verbal abuse in my direction. A new assertiveness was beginning to take hold, and one day I had had enough. Rather than ignoring the abuse, I advanced on them, confronting the ringleader and his cronies. I asked him what his problem was. Yes, I knew very well that this boy was my brother. Did he think I was so stupid that I kept forgetting and needed to be constantly reminded? Could he and I agree on the facts so that he would not need to keep yelling them at me abusively? There was little response, but he seemed to take my point.

This ringleader, however, was persistent. As he no longer wished for me to accost him at school in front of his friends, he took to yelling obscene names at me from a distance in public places, usually across parks, ovals or shopping centre car parks. One day he walked into the shop where I worked as a cashier. I decided it was time for another show down.

'Do you have something to say to me?' I asked.

He looked surprised and uncomfortable. 'Um, no.' he muttered.

'Well, that's funny, because you're always yelling something at me from a distance. The trouble is, I can't hear you properly. It's much more polite to speak to a person face to face. So if you have anything to say, I suggest you say it now.'

He apparently did not have anything to say. He slunk out of the shop. He stopped yelling abuse at me from that day on. It confirmed my suspicion that most bullies were simply cowards who needed confronting. Bullies no longer frightened me; they enraged and emboldened me.

The following year I did poorly on a Mathematics exam. The teacher had failed to mark and return the pre-exam assignment used for exam preparation, and ignored my objections. When I complained about this to my mother, she rang the Maths Department on my behalf. The Department consulted my teacher who said this was not true; I had already received my assignment back. I was furious. Being disadvantaged in a Maths test is one thing. Being accused of lying about it by the authority figure responsible is quite another. I confronted the teacher the following day, letting her know how angry I was to be misrepresented as a liar. The Maths Department later sent my parents the missing assignment.

These formative events and my responses to them would lead - in future years - to confrontations that were potentially more dangerous. They would also prepare me to one day confront the workers with the things that get under my skin the most – bullying, intimidation and lying.

One thing I did not confront in these early adolescent years was the existence of other Christians. Even from the inside of our cloistered little way of life, the reality of other self-proclaimed 'Christians' out there in the world was hard to deny. I certainly wondered about them, and their presence made me most uncomfortable. I learnt to avoid this issue the same way you learn not to look directly at the sun, lest it harm you. Just as you quickly shut your eyes and look away from the sun, so the mind belonging to a cult enacts thought-stopping techniques and quickly turns to alternative thoughts. We were constantly exhorted not to entertain any fears or doubts about The Way. *I must not give the devil a foothold* was the most tried and true thought-stopping phrase. It was used to prevent further thought about anything that could lead to doubting of any kind. *We have the one true ministry* was the next best consoling thought.

The spiritual themes I received from the religion of my youth were repeated and confirmed continually. Outside of The Way I would be eternally condemned. I could not be saved apart from it. If I did not listen to the workers I was not listening to God, and would be rebelling against Him.

These themes supposedly assured us of the safety of our souls if we remained within The Way. In reality, they did little to ease my very real and terrible fear of dying. We were continually told to ready ourselves for death; it would be terrible to die if we were not yet 'ready'. We had to make ourselves clean and renounce sin from our lives for this big event. Where did I stand? I knew I was not ready! I had a dreadful feeling that if I died God would have no reason to let me enter heaven. Was I good enough? Was I saved if I did not consciously sin today? What would happen if I sinned tomorrow? I remember wondering if I could be ready by the age of 70 or 80. I would definitely need at least that much time to have enough practise at being good so that I could sustain it for long enough to be saved.

We were told continually that God wanted us to be perfect, or at the very least to do our 'best' so that he could be pleased with us. Was I doing enough? Jesus was constantly upheld as the one who *lived to show us how to live, to be our perfect example*. I heard those words so many times, and wondered why he had to die a cruel death on a cross. Couldn't he have lived the same life and died a different way? I was also told he died for my sins, but this did not make sense. How could his dying possibly save me? After all, it was belonging to The Way and walking in the footsteps of Jesus that was far more important than His death and resurrection.

One of the Chosen Few
1990

*The Kingdom of God is founded in the world by the mutual
sacrifice of God's servants and of God's saints. The progress and
growth of this Kingdom depends upon our continued willingness,
as the servants and saints of God, to sacrifice. Earthly kingdoms are
founded by selfishness; God's heavenly Kingdom here upon earth is
founded by sacrifice.*

- Jack Carroll, US Worker, www.tellingthetruth.info

Despite some doubts and misgivings, I 'professed'
in The Way when I was 16 years old, entitling me to
take part in fellowship meetings on Sunday mornings. My
peers had generally professed several years earlier
between the ages of 12 and 14. Some profess even as
young as 8 or 10. I was not ready at that age, and not
keen to profess for the sake of appearances, being
determined to wait until I felt called by God. When I
did eventually profess, I struggled to fit in as a
member, feeling inexperienced compared to my peers.
Nevertheless, I genuinely felt I had made a decision to
serve God and commit my life to him.

At the time of publicly *making my choice*, I was
unprepared for and startled by the emotional response
of other members, who cried as they congratulated me
after the meeting, telling me I would never regret this
decision. A public profession of faith is made when a
gospel meeting is *tested*, which usually occurs once or
twice a year. A worker requests that 'those who would
like to indicate their choice to follow Jesus in this Way'
stand to their feet during the final verse of a selected
hymn. The emotional excitement of someone *making
their choice* is followed up by an excited round of

telephone calls to relatives to share the good news. Then begins the long road of proving one's self worthy of baptism, a process that may take up to several years.

In home fellowship meetings, where 5-15 professing members gather on a Sunday morning, proceedings are very formal. Cars pull up and park outside a suburban home. Members generally do not speak or greet one another when they arrive, coming in silently through an unlocked front door and settling into one of the chairs laid out in a circular pattern in the lounge room. Such quietness contributes to the *spirit* of the meeting. This *spirit* is a type of impersonal force, a vibe, which comes and goes as the worthiness of the gathering dictates. It is like a timid butterfly, which can be coaxed to descend on the gathering, but will just as quickly lift and flutter away if anything is done that is not conducive to the *right spirit*.

Moments tick by, often audibly from an old clock somewhere, until the meeting proper is announced. Everyone continues to be completely still and silent unless standing or kneeling to pray, or speaking his or her part in testimony. The decorum of the meeting is maintained at all times, even if something highly unusual occurs. A strange event may evoke a few slyly exchanged glances or a muffled giggle or snort, but meeting participants will not break with procedure in any way once a meeting has commenced.

Friends of mine were in a gospel meeting when someone towards the front of the hall died fairly early in the service. It was indicated that an ambulance should be called, and startled paramedics were ushered quietly up the external aisle to remove the body from the relevant row while the worker continued to preach without pausing. I have heard similar stories of deaths, strokes and other medical incidents occurring during a home meeting, gospel meeting or convention meeting, where the affected (or deceased) person was not assisted or dealt with until the meeting had concluded. The sad reality is that very few people would dare step outside the mandated protocol to interrupt a meeting without the express permission of a worker. Workers are unlikely to concede that anything is as important as a meeting in process; the meetings are revered above all else.

In the home fellowship meetings, each *professing* person is expected to deliver a short prayer (1-2 minutes each, in random turn), and then *give their testimony*, a verse from the Bible with personal insight (about 1-5 minutes each). Everyone is expected to take part every time; failure to speak or pray during the meeting would be noted by others present (a possible indication of a troubled spirit). After a meeting, members are encouraged to depart quickly, and not linger to chat. Too much socialising is actively discouraged; the *spirit of the meeting* will not remain long if you turn to talking together casually. If you depart quickly, you may *retain the spirit* of the meeting longer before *the cares of this world* again press in on you. In reality, it was probably also useful for preventing anything said during the meeting being queried, clarified or discussed afterwards. *The cares of this world* is a phrase used to shield against all earthly or fleshly matters, including moral and ethical issues or causes for justice. Spiritual matters only are emphasized, while practical matters are downgraded to a mere annoyance that distracts from this more important business of being spiritually minded.

Testimony time could be abused. If you had a grudge or accusation against a person in your meeting, your testimony could be aimed at them in a thinly veiled disguise. Friends and workers alike use this form of communication as an effective public rebuke, against which there is little opportunity for recourse.

I found speaking and praying in meetings very difficult to become accustomed to, and could not speak without notes. I found it hard to have *inspirations* for testimony, and did not understand much of the Scriptures, despite having attended up to four meetings a week every year of my life. I did not pray publicly in the meetings for more than a year, prompting a worker to tell me I had to try, at least. It is typical for everyone to pray in old English *('We thank Thee, Father…)*. As the (old) King James Version of the Bible is used almost exclusively, it somehow seemed logical that one would converse with God in old English as well.

The concept of prayer within the Two-by-Twos is peculiar. Designated as being strictly for spiritual matters only, the recipe varies little from the staple ingredients of thankfulness for The Way and the workers, concluding with a request to be *made more worthy* or *found more faithful.* The prayers are inevitably formulaic, predictable:

'Our Heavenly Father, I thank thee that we can come apart from the world, and be found today in this quiet place. We thank thee that thou hast revealed to us thy Way, and for thy servants. We pray that thou wouldst make us more worthy of this calling, and that we would be found faithful.'

Intoned solemnly and rhythmically, experienced voices of both testimony and prayer speak at a higher than natural monotone pitch, before dropping to a low note on the last word of each phrase. When one considers that the words spoken in the meetings tend to be almost artificially rendered, it is perhaps not so unusual that members do not casually speak of spiritual matters or pray together outside of meetings.

It was unthinkable to pray publicly for anyone by name, healing from sickness, safety in travel, world disasters or personal needs. Workers ridiculed Christians who prayed for *earthly matters*. I recall one particular sermon when a worker spoke on the evils of such ridiculous prayers, speaking with scorn and conviction of the horror he felt when he found out things that a particular couple had prayed for concerning their situation in life. Their ultimate sin had been their request to God for a child.

Even significant world events are of no import in the world of the Two-by-Twos. Some remember being at convention in the USA in September 2001 when the World Trade Centre twin towers fell in that unprecedented terrorist attack. The workers did not make the slightest mention of it as they addressed their congregation in the hours and days afterwards.

This emphasis on the spiritual at the expense of the physical comes at a high price. As I got older myself, I realised that the workers seemed completely oblivious to - or unwilling to address - the many pressures experienced by teenagers. Young people often did go out and do all the things they had been forbidden to do - with no restraint, guidance or discretion. Some did not know the meaning of self-control or how to exercise personal restraint, as sin was barely taught as a concept. Only the 'rules' were constantly reinforced as important. Much was stressed about the length and styling of a woman's hair, but nothing about sex. Many of my peers simply indulged in their desires, having little moral judgement. Keeping up appearances kept everyone happy; what was unseen didn't seem to hurt anyone.

Sexual conduct was certainly an issue rarely - if ever - discussed by the workers, unless it involved marriage, divorce or remarriage not sanctioned by them. They preferred not to address any matters of the flesh. We suspected it was wrong to engage in sexual relations outside of marriage, but the silence of the workers resulted in a lack of any clear conviction. I grew very disillusioned when I saw some of my peers engaging in sexual promiscuity in relationships that lasted only a few weeks, some of them teenagers much too young to marry. The issue had long been swept under the carpet and was rarely even spoken about, let alone challenged. The Way was about higher spiritual understanding, and did little to help in practical everyday living, dismissively referred to as *the cares of this life*.

Some of us knew that one young man had a girlfriend outside of The Way for the purpose of a sexual relationship, while he pursued other relationships within The Way for the purpose of marriage. He was a professing member, his fellowship seemingly unaffected by his immoral conduct outside the sphere of The Friends. We knew that another young unmarried couple rented motel rooms together, where they could have the added benefit of watching TV for the weekend. These, of course, were in-house secrets among the young people. Such actions caused others to question why they should even bother to abstain when so many others freely indulged without obvious consequence. It was a startling example to me of the repercussions of a ministry that depended on blind obedience to its own agenda rather than sound teaching and guidance from the Word of God.

There was one deep, dark fear that quaked almost universally in the breast of young people in The Way - 'Is it my calling to be a worker?' To become a worker was undoubtedly the highest calling; marriage and family was second best. It was a recurring theme of worker preaching - the aim to convict many a young heart to be *willing to forsake all* and *offer for the work*. It resulted in much secret guilt derived from privately knowing that we indeed were unwilling. Most of us wanted a romantic relationship, marriage and family. My guilt was perhaps less than some. As I was unaware of any workers on either side of my family (though apparently I do have some), I seemed genetically predisposed as non-worker material. I certainly did not hear any suggestion of it from my own parents.

Some families, however, brought forth and raised their children with great expectations, churning out a continuous supply of new worker heirs apparent. Some abdicated, but many fulfilled their calling. They were joined in their earnest service by many who were of less noble birth - the zealous new convert, the socially awkward, the sexually confused, the significant sinner seeking to do extra penance for wrongdoing, the narcissist seeking to be worshipped as a worker. It will be of no surprise to learn that *being in the work* has been a traumatic experience for many.

The Way, The Truth and The Lie

I consider that we are the most privileged people in all the world for the simple reason that what we believe and stand for and teach doesn't have its origin with man. You don't go back into the history of the world to find it. You have to go back to the beginning and to God. God had this plan in His heart and mind before the foundations of the world were laid.

- Arthur Boyce, Worker, Silverdale B.C. Conv. 6 Aug 1961
www.tellingthetruth.info

The first year I professed, while holidaying on a school break with my grandparents, I came across *The Secret Sect* by Doug & Helen Parker. An avid reader who spent most of my holidays curled in a corner with a book, it is little wonder I discovered it on their bookshelf. It was an extraordinary expose of the foundations of the Two-by-Two church, with detailed references and witnesses.

Doug, a former member, had intended to enter the Two-by-Two ministry in his youth. Then he stumbled across a dark secret about the true origins of this group that claimed to be apostolic, continuous from the time of Jesus. The truth was far less extraordinary. It had a recent beginning. It had a human founder, a self-proclaimed prophet.

I read with disbelief and horror the allegations that my church, the One True Way - the church with no founder except Christ - actually started not that long ago. A Scotsman named William Irvine had originated it in 1897 in Ireland.

A mental earthquake shook the very foundations of my faith. Massive cracks of doubt splayed through all that I knew and trusted. Up until that time, I had truly believed in everything I had been told. We were different, specifically because we were not just another church started by a man or group of men. We had *no earthly founder* or *doctrines of men*, only the direct teachings of Jesus passed down from the original New Testament ministry. The workers *were* the ongoing lineage of the New Testament ministry. They stated this emphatically and authoritatively. It was at the core of our belief system. Our Way came *from the shores of Galilee*. The cold hard claims of this book, so far removed from everything I had been taught, prompted a reaction of immediate denial and disgust.

'This guy reckons that a man named William Irvine started The Way,' I scoffed to Nana. Shock started to set in when she did not deny it.

'Well, sometimes God has to raise up a man to restore his true way again.' she replied carefully. It was the first of many explanations I was to hear from workers scrambling to respond to queries about William Irvine.

As the full implications of this discovery started to seep into my consciousness over the following days, I felt as though I was trying to recover from a heavy blow to the gut. It had knocked the wind out of me, and it still hurt to breathe. I could not understand why I had never known this before, why I had never heard it even mentioned. Did the workers know and not tell people, deliberately trying to deceive them? Did they not know themselves? I had always equated the workers with being far above any form of falsehood. Yet here I was, faced with the knowledge that I had been - apparently - purposely and consistently deceived by the entire hierarchy of my church. It seemed like a bizarre and complex conspiracy where every worst fear is realised. The cracks of doubt threatened to widen into chasms, and I was precariously balanced, fearful that any thought in the wrong direction would cause my whole belief system to split wide open.

And yet I could not bring myself to fully acknowledge that I had been deceived. I desperately wanted to believe that Nana's rationalisation was at least a plausible explanation. This was the single foundation of faith I possessed; beneath was only the dark, dank earth of unbelief. Despite having read only a small portion, I closed the book and closed my mind. I quickly erected a 'do not enter' sign, and retreated to safer parts of the foundation. Surely The Way still had the only true form of ministry, even if it was not from the beginning. Maybe the book was not even true. I paved over the cracks with compliance and conformity. My efforts were so convincing that even I forgot that the foundation of my faith had been so severely compromised. I would not come back to that book for some years.

I made a conscious decision at this time to turn my eyes away from that which I did not want to know. I truly believed in The Way. I had grown up in it, been taught what to believe, and lived by a deeply ingrained code of conduct. I was a child of The Truth, as were my family, relatives and friends, and my whole childhood had been lived as one of these *special people*. Every cord of existence bound me tightly and firmly to the group.

Being in a cult is not just about being controlled by a set of rules given by the hierarchy. The rules had become my own value system, an integral part of myself, the code by which I lived. To mentally or physically separate myself from the group was not just about disobeying the authority figures. It was something much more profound - I would be breaking my own code, my own belief system. I could not violate my own conscience, my own integrity by doing things forbidden - not just by the workers, but forbidden by my own sense of being, who I was in the most profound sense.

Most of us would not think of purposely going and killing someone. It would go against every fibre of our being; it is criminally wrong and ethically immoral. Religious systems build up the same muscles of restraint as moral conviction; to step outside them is to break our own convictions in a fundamental and damaging way. To break the beliefs I now owned for myself would destroy who I was. I would become someone else. Someone I did not recognise. Someone estranged from my family and friends. I could not conceive of becoming an outsider, just some person *out there in the world*.

Consequently, when anything of this nature threatened my faith, I learned to erect another roadblock. The ongoing and constant conditioning of the meetings was simple yet deeply effective. *We are the one true way. We have the one true ministry. We are the only true messengers of God.* The constant preaching to this effect had now achieved sufficient momentum from meeting attendance and conformity to propel me inexorably onwards.

Thus was my life when I entered college at the age of 16 and first laid eyes on David.

A Swooping Magpie
1991 – 1992

The great enemy of the truth is very often not the lie - deliberate, contrived and dishonest - but the myth - persistent, persuasive and unrealistic. Too often we hold fast to the clichés of our forebears. We subject all facts to a prefabricated set of interpretations. We enjoy the comfort of opinion without the discomfort of thought.

- John F. Kennedy

After seeing David in English class that first time, I proceeded to avoid him as much as possible. Occasionally I would turn up to class with several friends and find him sitting at 'our' table, an event I would find particularly irritating. He was always alone and didn't seem to know anyone, but that was not my problem. We were put into a discussion group together at one stage, and I was rude and abrupt to him (it seemed a sure-fire way to prevent any possible future marriage). At one stage, we had to do a presentation on a television show of choice. I didn't want to admit that this created a problem for me, so I did enough research on a show to contribute something to a group presentation. David, apparently not familiar with most of the popular shows of the time either, chose to give an individual presentation on why he did not watch television. It was the most memorable presentation of the class. It also made me very uneasy.

As time went on, I could not resist looking for him wherever I went, and was always very aware of his presence. The task of trying to ignore David was slowly becoming a full time - and failing - preoccupation. The more I tried to avoid him and not think about him, the more I knew I was constantly thinking of him. This situation continued for some months. Eventually, I was thinking about him almost every waking moment. It was becoming beyond ridiculous. His face began to appear before me wherever I went. When I walked to school, when I went to meetings, when I sat down to play the piano, when I knelt down to pray at night. My frustration became intense. Trying to ignore this internal pressure was like trying to ignore myself. I could not escape from my mind, and my mind could not escape from thinking about that one person I did not want anything to do with. I did not confide in anyone. Finally, some friends at school pulled me aside.

'Liz, something is going on with you. Whatever it is, it's eating away at you.' They implored me to do something about it.

Shocked by their observation, I still said nothing. I was not prepared to acknowledge even to myself what was happening, let alone to anyone else. But their comments made me realise that this state of affairs wasn't diminishing, and that this strange involuntary obsession needed to be dealt with. I finally raised it with God. I already prayed regularly, daily, but this had been the elephant in the room, the issue I refused to raise. Now I finally asked him to take it away.

'Please Lord, take this person out of my mind, I can't concentrate on anything else, and I don't want anything to do with him'. As soon as I started talking to God about it, he seemed to answer immediately, telling me I must talk to David. I don't mean that I heard a voice from heaven. I didn't. I had a sudden, strong and insistent urging that I must talk to David, like a heavy pressure bearing down on my being. Was this really from God, this insistence? I had no real way of knowing. It made no sense from the perspective of all I knew and believed. Rule number 1 – do not get involved with an outsider. I ignored the insistent urging and kept asking for David to be taken away from my thoughts and mind. This burden on my soul became heavier and heavier the more I prayed, and yet I persisted for weeks with the same request – 'Lord, please take this away from me.'

At some point I realised this pressure would not be taken away, and started to tackle it head on. I finally acknowledged this request as being from God, and said no.

'No, Lord, I will not speak to this person. I don't want anything to do with him. No, no, no.' But the pressure remained unbelievably persistent. I eventually had to admit defeat. Well, not quite. I attempted a different direction.

'Why? What am I going to say? "Hi, God wants me to talk to you?" Lord, this can't seriously be what you want me to do.' This was ridiculous, and I told God so. But the pressure only continued to intensify.

After a long battle of nearly eight months, God won. I was spiritually and mentally worn out. In a desperate and angry prayer I said 'Fine - I'll talk to him. But I have absolutely nothing to say, so this is all up to you.' I knew exactly where David would be the next day; our paths would cross between buildings as we changed classes. 'Lord, I'll be there, do what you want!'

And so it was a fine day on the 16th of September 1991 when I finally and unwillingly came face to face with David as promised. As we neared one another, I saw he had blood all over the side of his face, and a wound in the side of his nose. My cue was not only obvious, but unavoidable.

'What on earth happened to you?' I asked. Of all the 'talk to David' scenarios I had imagined, this was the most unscripted, but he seemed willing to talk to me. A magpie - one of those distinctive black and white Australian birds that become highly aggressive during breeding season - had swooped and attacked him that morning as he rode to school, and he had not had a chance to clean the blood from his face as he was already late for class. I asked him to have lunch with me, and he readily agreed. I was stunned by the straightforwardness of it all, and especially David's seeming lack of surprise. He met me for lunch in an art classroom where I was working on some fabric design, and it seemed as though my request had been perfectly normal, even though we had hardly ever spoken two sentences to each other in our lives. We talked for a solid hour, about anything and everything.

The next day I was walking home from school across the oval when I heard a voice calling my name from behind. David caught up with me, and pushed his bike to accompany me all the way home. From that time on we saw each other every day. David would always walk me home, and often walk me to school as well. We lived in the same direction away from college, less than two kilometres apart. My best friend had developed a chronic fatigue type of illness and had to drop out of school for the remainder of the year, so there were few times that David and I were not together in our free time.

One of the very first conversations we had, only one or two days after the magpie incident, was about Christianity. David brought up the subject very quickly, most likely to see if I had any church background. I explained the basic set-up of the 'church' I attended as best I could.

I was most interested to learn that he called himself a Christian. Suddenly it all seemed obvious. So this was the plan! Perhaps I had been given the divine task of bringing about David's conversion to the *one true way*. I already knew he didn't watch television – it seemed a perfect fit.

I was now both intrigued and cautious. I still did not believe for one moment that this was the man I was going to marry one day, and still definitely did not intend to mention my crazy imaginings to anyone, least of all David. Besides, I didn't want to marry him. Not only was I not attracted to him at all, but I had a serious romantic obsession with a guy from The Way; I'd had a crush on him for nearly two years.

Despite every intention to the contrary, somehow David and I became best friends. We spent every free moment at college together, and talked for many hours a day. We walked to and from school. We continued to talk about church occasionally, but it was not explored much further. I did not yet want to ask David to a gospel meeting, and certainly could not attend his church. David eventually took me home to meet his family, and he met my family. I think both sets of parents were extremely cautious, although we were not involved in any acknowledged romantic relationship at this time. My parents were understandably wary, lest I get involved with an outsider.

There was another reason for their consternation - one of the professing men from our gospel meeting had shown an interest in me and taken me out. But some first dates are destined for disaster, and this one fell definitively into such a category. He was new in town, older and employed. I was still in school. He had not even registered on my radar as a romantic interest when I suddenly found myself on the phone one summer afternoon, being asked out on a date. The shrill ringing had awoken me from an afternoon nap, and, groggy and disoriented, I somehow agreed to have dinner with him before I even knew what was happening. The regret started the moment I replaced the receiver. Not a promising start.

On the night in question we walked into the agreed restaurant to be confronted with a whole table of other young friends from our gospel meeting, who immediately engaged in much hilarity at having 'sprung' us on a date, or possibly even 'outed' us as a couple. In the awkwardness of this completely unexpected and embarrassing predicament, they invited us to join them, and I accepted. The night did not end well. I knew this gentleman felt he had not had a fair innings, but as I had no interest in him whatsoever, I politely declined to see him again in a romantic context. I later heard that he believed I had set him up by knowing that The Friends would be at that restaurant that particular night. Nothing could have been further from the truth – I was mortified by the situation.

When I brought David home, my mother immediately concluded that he was the reason I had refused further dates. Several times she suggested that I should go out with the young man again, and at least give him a chance. She even invited him over for dinner, which happened to be on the same night I had invited David for dinner. They both came, a situation that was more than a little awkward. I just couldn't bring myself to go out with him again. Even though he seemed to tick all the right boxes in terms of being an eligible bachelor from The Way, it was like the repelling side of magnetism at work.

This had happened to me a year earlier in another relationship with a young man whom I had met at convention. He was kind and friendly, and very keen on me, and I felt an obligation to try to make it work. A repelling force was strongly in play, so strongly that I felt physically nauseous in his presence. After some months of growing unease, and failure to quell the sick sensation in the pit of my stomach that something was terribly wrong, I had to concede that I could not make this relationship work, no matter how hard I tried.

There was only one boy who I liked immensely, who was a prospect for a real relationship. We went to high school together, and in our final year, I knew his interest in me was increasing. I managed to avoid his advances by making it clear that I was seeing someone else. It was true, but also a most timely and convenient decoy. He was too nice, and I liked him too much. He was an outsider, and I was not willing to risk falling in love with him, which would threaten my faith.

And yet here now was David, also an outsider, completely unsuitable, no romantic attraction on my part whatsoever, and yet I was being pulled towards him by some curiously inexplicable, irresistible force.

David's family was very surprised, to say the least, when I was introduced to their household, late in 1991. He is one of six siblings, five boys and a girl – in that order. David is the third boy. I got the distinct feeling that no one was expecting him to bring a girl home, though one of his older brothers had seen us together at college. The Coleman household soon became a second home to me, though much curiosity abounded concerning the church I attended, and what we believed. It was also a source of surprise to them that I had such an aversion to attending their church's youth group. I did go to youth group with David a few times in the New Year, but my parents were strongly opposed to this new development.

A Different Spirit

1992

They want to call themselves Christian without adhering to the tenets of the historic 'doctrinal' faith. They change the major core teachings to mean something other than they are defined in the Bible and by the history of the church. The cults do not agree with the historic (Biblical) Christian faith.

- www.letusreason.org

In the New Year, the subject of church came up again more prominently. I invited David to *gospel meetings* when they commenced again (having stopped over summer for conventions), to which he came and seemed to find interesting. He also pressed me to accompany him to his church. This was out of the question. I knew my parents would not allow it, and I believed there was no point. The more David pressed on this issue, the more agitated I became. He had quickly become aware of the fact that my church considered itself exclusive. He set about trying to explain the doctrine of his protestant church to me, and the history of the Reformation that led to it. I stoutly refused to listen, declaring only that he did not understand - my church came directly from the apostles, and the Reformation had nothing to do with us.

David was quickly discovering that while my church appeared genuine on the outside, something was very wrong. He had several discussions with the preachers separately, and grew more concerned when he received very different answers to the same question. The preachers began to view him as a problem, which put a good deal of pressure on me to end our friendship. I in turn pressured David to attend meetings with me, and he grew more confused. He soon made the decision to start attending profession of faith classes again at his own church to reaffirm what he believed and why.

Things came to a head one Monday lunch time at college when David decided to share his concerns about my church. I immediately became very defensive, and deeply wounded by his criticisms. He said that he had now attended a number of church services with me, and listened to many shallow sermons. Shallow? I did not understand what he meant, as it was the only preaching I had ever heard. The next thing he said was especially surprising.

'I am very worried about who they think Jesus is' he said.

'The Son of God, of course', I replied. Who else would he be?

'But is he the Son of God, or God the Son?' David persisted. 'I know it sounds very subtle, but there is a difference.' Now I was very confused; I had never heard the expression 'God the Son' before. David tried to explain the concept of God in three persons as Father, Son and Holy Spirit, which I rejected immediately. It did not make sense, and certainly went against everything I had ever known.

'I asked your ministers this question separately,' David said after a while, 'and I got two different answers. One agreed with me, and the other one didn't.'

I became distraught, accusing David of not being willing to accept the gospel, of trying to destroy my faith in it, and goodness knows what else. David, being the gentleman he was, asked if I would like to go home, and accompanied me. All the way home I cried and poured out many things I had heard from the workers over the years. I kept asserting that we knew we were right, we were the only church, and if he was willing to believe, he would know it too. David mostly just listened, but did say several pointed things about my beliefs. We parted at my driveway both very upset. As he walked away, I truly believed that our friendship was over. David later told me that as he walked home that evening he stepped out straight in front of a car and only just missed being hit, such was the turmoil of his mind.

I was sobbing heartily by the time I got to the front door, and collapsed in my mother's arms as I described what had happened. My mother was very indignant at the things David had said, though had no explanations for some of the issues he had raised. She did state very firmly that I was better off without him. I went straight to bed and stayed there for fifteen hours, refusing to go to college the next morning.

At that time, we had gospel meetings on Tuesday nights in a school hall. When my family and I went to the meeting that next night, I started shaking when I saw David's car already in the parking lot. My family was also very surprised, but pleased.

'I'm sorry, I didn't realize how badly upset you were over this' he said after the meeting. He had been worried when I had not attended classes that day.

When I relayed these events to the workers several days later, they seemed to think that David was making good progress, and assured me I had acted in all the right ways. However, they obviously detected I was in a dangerous position, as a number of 'visits' to my parents' house ensued.

I broached the subject of 'The Secret Sect' with them on one of these visits, and the workers were very anxious to dispel the terrible myths and lies of this devilish book. They described the writer as being very bitter towards The Way, someone who was accepted as a worker, but had then wanted to go and spend all his money on a big holiday before going into the work, rather than *forsaking all*. They claimed the author had written the book in retaliation for not being permitted to enter *the work*. They were noncommittal on the origins of the group, carefully avoiding it to focus instead on the vengeful nature of the author. Their language had also changed subtly. They now referred to The Way as being *as it was in the beginning*, rather than *from the beginning*. Over time, I was made to believe that they had never claimed apostolic origin – this was just a figment of my imagination. God had raised up his true Way again, and that was what mattered. Much later, I was consoled to discover that many others felt as deceived as I had. It was not just my imagination or misunderstanding, but rather a deception in common.

The workers also told me they had been called 'Cooneyites' by outsiders, but they explicitly denied that they were Cooneyites, telling me that this was a completely separate group of people, following a man named Edward Cooney who did not belong to The Fellowship. This claim was technically correct, but very misleading and purposely deceptive. As I later discovered, Edward Cooney was indeed one of the founding members, but was eventually put out of the group, leaving with a faithful contingent. The current Cooneyites (who also deny any name) still exist to this day, I believe, as a small but separate group in several parts of the world, including Mildura in the state of Victoria (Australia).

Incidentally, this is my father's hometown. When Edward Cooney was put out of The Way in 1928 (at a special meeting of workers in Lurgan, Ireland), the workers also cast out those who continued to open their homes to him[3]. Within a few short months, instructions were sent across the globe that he was not to be admitted into The Fellowship anywhere in the world. His main 'sin' was refusing to submit to self-appointed overseers or limit his evangelism to the areas assigned him. He insisted on having liberty to preach wherever he felt led, not where he was told to go. He also continued to insist that he had originally come to Christ as a young man before meeting William Irvine, holding on to his faith as preceding the current 'only true ministry'.

Despite being an outcast, the incorrigible Cooney continued to preach all the remaining days of his life. In response to further schisms within The Fellowship in Australia, Cooney eventually travelled there to visit outcasts in several states. His final days were spent in Mildura, where he maintained a loyal band of supporters until his death in 1960. My father was 16 years old by this time, and had a keen awareness of the presence of Edward Cooney in that country town as *he whose name must not be spoken.*

'I tell people that the only "coney" I know about is the little creature mentioned in the Old Testament' (Lev. 11:5, Deu. 14:7) laughed one of the workers to me on the night of our discussion. I later learned that this was a standard line response to any queries about Edward Cooney.[4]

At the invitation of the workers, David came around to our house to hear them explain more fully about The Way. They gave testimonies of their experiences, claiming that they were *led by the Spirit* in everything they did and everywhere they went. They claimed not to be assigned to go anywhere, in fact they weren't really even part of an organisation. Rather, they just *followed the Spirit* who told them where to go and where they would preach next. David was more than sceptical.

'They don't follow the Spirit.' he said to me firmly. 'They're told where to go. They are an organisation and it is organised who will go where.' He was not having a bar of their mystical assertions, and was perplexed as to why they would try to claim otherwise. Why the deception?

It is with true irony that I now look upon this claim, knowing that clinging to this prerogative was the core reason why Cooney was excommunicated. He was far less of a hypocrite. The current day workers continue to pay lip service to this ideal, while obeying the orders of their superiors without question; going where they are told.

Unbeknownst to me, David invited the workers around to his own house to talk with them on two other separate occasions. As these instances were more than a year apart, he spoke with a different pair the second time, when his father was also present, who took the opportunity to question them as well. His parents had attended a gospel meeting to investigate this group I was involved with, and which their son was occasionally attending.

When David told me about their first visit to his house, I was most surprised, and anxious to find out from the workers how it had gone. I caught up with one of them at a fellowship picnic, and asked for some feedback. The worker seemed preoccupied, but spoke to me hurriedly.

'Yes, yes, I regret to tell you that David is not making good progress. He asks too many questions and does not seem to be very accepting of the truth. But, you're young and attractive, and you won't be left on the shelf.'

He took off abruptly, leaving me to work through his response. It took a moment to realise the implications of what he had said; clearly, I was being told to give David up. Of course, this wasn't said directly, but if I had the right spirit, I would fully appreciate his meaning. Picking up hints and hidden meanings from the workers and acting on them proved that you had the spirit.

It was more than a year later that David invited the second pair of workers to his house to talk privately with them. After that conversation one of them approached me to reiterate that things did not look good.

'He has been deeply indoctrinated with other beliefs, and it is our opinion that such indoctrination would take several years to reverse, if ever' one said. David was obviously a lost cause, and I must give him up. The future was starting to look extremely bleak. For by now I had fallen in love for the first time, and fallen hard, with someone I could not have, could not convert, and for whom I could not leave the only true way.

Life became much more difficult from this point. David and I were able to spend happy interludes together, but only if we ignored for a time the underlying problems of personal faith. We were very aware of the fact that our relationship was likely doomed, but could not resist enjoying each other's company. We both despaired and grieved privately in our own ways. David considered many times ending the relationship, but each time something seemed to hold him back and prevent him taking this step.

When alone, I spent most of my time in utter confusion and misery. The hopelessness of it all would descend on me in a thick black cloud that I could not penetrate. I was painfully aware of the fact that our relationship could not continue indefinitely on its present terms. Yet I could not end it either.

Many times I wanted to really try and explore the differences and beliefs of both churches, but my mind was trapped. I had been taught for many years not to listen to teachings of other churches. We were not to confuse our minds with doctrines of men, for such work was of the devil. If we listened he would surely win, brainwashing and luring us into eternal damnation. This was the way of obedience for The Fellowship. It was considered so dangerous to listen to other views of religion that we were taught to reject them by default, without thought or consideration. I was therefore terrified to listen to whatever David tried to say. He later referred to me at this time as a brick wall he could not penetrate.

Throughout our relationship to this point, I managed to keep my mind tightly wrapped in the security of total obedience to The Way. But the more time I spent with David's family, the more unnerved and unsettled I became. They called themselves Christians, and were very committed to both family and church worship. Worse still, they acted like

Christians. With this evidence continually before me, it became harder and harder to justify why my church was right and theirs was wrong.

A certain incident around this time caused me significant unease. I was visiting at David's one day when his older brother Jeremy described a recent near miss involving his car and another vehicle. The other driver had acted recklessly, endangering both their lives in a narrowly avoided serious accident.

'I could have died!' said Jeremy. 'I mean, it wouldn't worry me, I know where I'm going, but what about the other driver?'

I comprehended but could not quite cope with his comment. How could he be so sure about where he was going when he died? I had never heard such a thought expressed. From all I knew and had been taught, none of us could ever be certain. Ever. How arrogant is it to say that you have been a good enough person to meet God and not be afraid? I believed that salvation apart from The Way was impossible. This family seemed far more sure of their faith than anyone I had ever met in the Two-by-Twos, including the workers.

Somewhere deep in the back of my consciousness, nagging thoughts kept surfacing. Had I ever been allowed to think and work these things out for myself? Why were the workers so opposed to the questions I asked? Such thoughts were immediately subdued most of the time, in fear of disobeying God and angering him with my unbelief. My frustration mounted, and became unbearable. I was not a puppet; I wanted to unlock my mind and be allowed to think freely. I wanted to set about finding out the truth - whatever it might be, and become finally convinced one way or the other. I wanted to discover truth for myself - through learning, discernment and revelation together. My mind became restless and I was plagued by doubts of every kind. There was no longer anything of which I was completely certain. I began to have a recurring image of standing before the throne of God, saying 'Lord, I have done as I was told and believed in this church, your only true way!' God did not welcome me.

'By who were you told this?' he would always reply. The answer terrified and haunted me. Could I trust the workers and everything they said? Did God know and recognise them as his own? Would God save me because I had believed in them?

I continued to have this image many times, and expressed something about this with my grandmother one day.

'Nana, if we do not go to other churches, how do we know we are the only ones who are right? We don't know what other churches teach and believe. Isn't it a bit dangerous just to believe whatever you are told and not look into it for yourself?'

Nana explained that we knew we were the only right ones because we had the only real ministry that came from Jesus. We didn't have to look at other churches to learn that. I was not satisfied.

'But people are born into other sects and religions who believe they are the only right ones. What will happen to those people if they always do what they are told and never look into it for themselves? How will they find out that we are the only true way?'

Nana seemed uncomfortable with this line of reasoning.

'God understands that people are in those situations, and will judge them accordingly.'

I was frustrated.

'But God will not excuse people who thought they were not allowed to think for themselves! Surely he gave us a mind to think, not to just blindly believe everything we are told!'

Nevertheless, I continued to profess, continuing on the treadmill of meetings, gospel meetings, conventions and special meetings. At the annual mid-year *special meeting*, a broad geographical region of meetings comes together for an all-day event with guest workers. Some of The Friends travel great distances to attend more than one special meeting a year. Some of my notes from the 1992 special meeting read:

'How sweet it is when weaned from all, we follow Jesus' secret call'⁵ We are gathered here today to follow the secret call of Jesus. The world cannot understand why, because it is secret, hidden. It is a call that we have come to know, and love, and we come here longing for it. In Samuel's time, God was finding it hard to find lives that would respond to his call. Then he found a young life, Samuel. We're glad for the time that we recognised God's call and responded. 'Speak, thy servant heareth' said Samuel. It is we who listen and understand the call to our hearts. Maybe others don't understand, and don't hear, but we do.

As usual, it was the constant refrain of being different, special, set apart from the rest of the world. Nobody understands, but we have a special knowledge that they don't. It was us against the world, insiders against outsiders, *friends* against *strangers*.

My notes for the opening of my last convention in 1992 read:

When the poor and needy seek water, and there is none, the Lord of Israel will hear their cry, and open rivers in high places⁶. But we need to seek, we need to be in a poor and needy condition. When we come apart, we are conscious of many failures over the past year. But there has not failed one word of all God promised. He will not fail or forsake us. The Lord wants to speak to our hearts, that it would have a deep, cleansing effect there. Job went through so many bad experiences, but at the end, he was able to say – 'I know thou'st can do everything'. There was a complete repentance, and crying to the Lord. Be poor, needy and seeking.

This is extremely typical of their overall preaching. It does not get any better or more in-depth than this. Workers generally start with a chosen theme (i.e., the theme here is to be *poor, needy and seeking*), and then string together a multitude of sentimental phrases to provide encouragement to continue in The Way. They will look for verses that seem to support their theme at face value, and pluck them out of context to quote in their preaching somewhere. For the example, the reference to Job takes a Biblical character and a generalisation about him (he went through so many bad experiences), and then completely misunderstands the Bible's actual representation of Job. Job was seeking vindication from the Lord, while his friends were insisting that he must have done something wrong, of which he was not repenting. Scripture is rarely expounded in context; it is primarily used as a stepping-stone to a series of worker-speak platitudes. These platitudes are designed to extract an emotional response from the hearer with the same never-ending theme to continue walking in The Way, and to become more like Jesus. While it may have been whetting the emotional appetite of other hearers, I was far more conscious of my own mind – a bare and neglected spiritual wasteland there at convention.

While the Bible is held in high esteem and is certainly read and used by members, a particular interpretation is strongly reinforced with a message that is apparently not obvious to other churches. Workers are the only ones qualified to explain the contents of the Bible, and interpret it. Perhaps most tellingly, members rarely take their Bible to gospel meetings. The common understanding is that the Bible is a dead book without the interpretation of the workers, so hearing them speak is given far more weight than reading the Bible for yourself. Some diligent members make it their business to take notes of entire sermons by workers – especially at the annual conventions – which are then typed up and distributed among the faithful. These notes are read again and again, assisting with getting the presence of the spirit outside of meetings. *Convention Gems* are collected and distributed, and are especially well loved – a *gem* is a phrase uttered by a worker which seems particularly profound. Such notes and gems are the nearest one can come to documented theology on the group (apart from their compilation of hymns in the 'Hymns Old & New' songbook, many of which are written by the workers).

Sermons may not be electronically or digitally recorded. The spirit, I was told many times while sitting under the preaching of the workers, does not operate through means of recording, which is like an artificial form of preaching. The spirit can only be caught from live preaching, passed on in the flesh. Moreover, the recordings may *fall into the wrong hands*, a sinister warning repeated often, leaving us to wonder whose hands those might be.

The workers are very sensitive about having their preaching scrutinised, and who can blame them? Their Biblical ignorance is often apparent. I do not say this to shame or mock them, but we need a reality check here. If one of The Friends feels *called to the work*, and subsequently *offers for the work* and is accepted, they are simply designated the title 'worker' and sent off to preach the following year. No form of preparation of any kind is undertaken apart from the selling of personal effects. The individual is not even questioned in any way as to their theological understanding. They are literally told to walk to the stage and start preaching, where they are greeted with a hushed reverence by many eyes gazing upon the newly ordained.

The workers subsequently learn to 'preach' by bouncing off random Bible verses as a stone skims across the top of a pond. Many of The Friends have not heard any other preaching in their life, and have no idea of the true Biblical scholarship required to plumb the depths of the Scriptures. The Friends are told – and truly believe – that the preaching they hear from the workers is exceptional and incomparable to anything that people hear in churches *out there in the world*. The workers constantly extol the virtues of their *simple and humble, lowly way,* even boasting about their lack of education. It seems imperative that they also keep their people as simple, humble and lowly as possible (preferably as uninformed and uneducated as themselves). To this end, higher education of any form tends to be viewed with suspicion or even actively discouraged.

Workers are extremely evasive about their doctrine, often being unwilling to meet and discuss issues when asked. They know their only real power lies in preaching – uninterrupted, unhindered one-sided rhetoric aimed at passive listeners who must continue listening until they *get* it – the esoteric knowing that this *is* the only true way. The workers have long learnt to avoid entering into reasoned, rational, theological argument, even in private. They rely on coercion and submission to their preaching. *Feeling* is valued far above thinking. *Knowing in your heart* that this is the *right way* is the important principle; the poor saps who go to Bible college to get their heads filled with useless theological knowledge are openly mocked. Why go to so much trouble thinking and learning when you can just *know* that you are right?

Hostility towards other professing Christians is very evident, with mainstream churches accused of having *false* ministers who are allegedly in ministry only for what they can get out of it. *False teachers* in *churches of the world* teach *doctrines of men* which are *from the devil*. As these false teachers receive a salary from the church, and a home to live in, their occupation, so I was told, is no different from that of a public servant or shop owner, who does his work and receives his wage. They are not true shepherds, but hirelings, worthy only of derision and scorn.

A worker through whom I professed walked up to me one day in the middle of the convention grounds. I was excited to see her, and pleasantly surprised at the privilege of having her approach me, for she had hardly ever spoken to me. I had heard of young people professing who then wrote letters to the worker through whom they professed, but it had not been my experience. She said hello, and then asked if I did any sewing. I was thrilled that she was taking such an interest in me, as sewing was my favourite hobby.

'Yes, lots!' I responded. I started to tell her about some of the projects I was undertaking, but she cut me off.

'Then you should sew something over the top of your dress' she said, indicating my chest. After a few more awkward words she turned and walked away. I was left standing there filled with shame and fury. These are the only words she speaks to me and this is what she chooses to say? I loved this dress. It had a wide scooped neckline, but it did not reveal anything untoward. Quite apart from this, the thing that stung most was that I realised she had no interest in me at all. She had only approached me to scold me on my choice of dress. If I had been wearing something quite 'faultless', she probably would not have bothered speaking to me.

---

[3] The excommunication of Edward Cooney is detailed in 'The Secret Sect' by Doug & Helen Parker (p.76) and 'The Life and Ministry of Edward Cooney' by Patricia Roberts (p.143)

[4] www.tellingthetruth.info/workers_early/jamiesons.php#elizabeth

[5] Reference to a hymn – 'How Sweet it is' – No 247, Hymns Old & New, R L Allan & Son

[6] Most likely a reference to Isaiah 41:18

Foreign Gods
1992 – 1993

Why do the nations say,
'Where is their God?'
Our God is in heaven;
he does whatever pleases him.
But their idols are silver and gold,
made by human hands.

- Psalm 115:2-4 [NIV]

As my college years drew to a close at the end of 1992, David and I grew closer. In the summer of 92-93, I went to Japan for 5 weeks on an exchange program. This was an interesting time of separation, not least because I was separated from both David and The Meetings, by some significant distance. There is nothing like geographical space to help gain perspective, and there were some interesting events that took place. In addition, I was staying in the home of complete strangers, a traditional Japanese family who were members of the exchange program to which I had applied. They were not part of The Way. They were not even Christians. In fact they worshipped a multitude of gods. Add to that a foreign culture and language, and I was light years away from everything I had ever known.

Firstly, I did meet up with some of The Friends over there, with whom I was put in contact before I left Australia. To the great concern of my Japanese host family, I took a train, alone, across this foreign country to meet up with a couple of female workers whom I did not know - an American and her younger Japanese companion - in the home of an American lady who had married a Japanese man, both of whom were in The Way. It was an enjoyable visit, although I committed a cultural faux pas by enthusiastically greeting and hugging the workers. The Japanese worker was quite shocked at my familiarity, and did not respond well.

It so happened that an Australian girl whom I had met at an aunt's wedding was in Japan at that time, also visiting the home of this *professing* couple, so we had a nice catch up. Although she did not discuss it with me, I knew from Two-by-Two talk that she had been married to a very violent man. The workers had insisted she keep returning to her abusive professing husband, which she did a number of times prior to finally leaving before she was permanently injured or killed. Unfortunately, she is not the only woman I know who nearly lost their life due to returning to a violent husband at the insistence of the workers.

The visit went quite well, and I gained an interesting insight into the life of a white woman living in Japan, where foreigners are considered outsiders. It was obvious that the Two-by-Twos were having a difficult time gaining ground in Japan, a country where people are far more familiar with multiple gods, idol worship and shrines. The older worker confided to me that the Jehovah's Witnesses and Mormons were gaining far more converts than The Way.

The religious climate in Japan was both fascinating and depressing. The temples were full of charms that could be bought for any and every purpose – from general good luck to cures of specific ailments. I began to see why they were called 'charms' – they charmed many a person and their money to part company. On the grounds of one Buddhist temple was a veritable shopping mall of gods in the form of large wooden statues; just pick the one you like best and focus your affections on it. If you don't get what you want, you can pick another one at a later date. Or keep your own personal coterie of gods; having more than one or two or three at a time didn't seem to be a problem. I observed that the streets were full of roadside shrines – statues set in small, purpose built huts with bowls of fresh water, fruit and flowers placed before them, symbols of regular devotion and appeasement.

I was beginning to understand a lot about idol worship. All of these gods were the result of fertile human minds, preying on the pockets and superstitions of their fellow man. These gods were also very convenient, there for the picking and choosing according to one's preferences – designer gods.

My Japanese host sister seemed to take full advantage of this religious smorgasbord. She burned incense at traditional Japanese temples, purchased charms from the Buddhist temple, and attended chapel mass at her private Catholic school. Certainly she saw no distinction between the Catholic faith and every other god on offer in her culture. When I had the opportunity to attend school with her for a few days, I saw why. Lining the hallways of her school were tall marble statues of 'saints', from which they were encouraged to pick one as a recipient of their prayers. I couldn't blame her for seeing no difference between picking a statue at school and picking a wooden statue from the temple marketplace.

During this time, I drew closer to God. I was shocked by the idol worship, and, while wanting to show respect to my host family as far as possible, drew the line at showing deference to other gods in any way.

For New Year's celebrations I was dressed - at the expense of my host family - in a kimono, complete with hair and headpiece, stockings and shoes. We were taken to a photographer, then proceeded on foot via mountain staircases to the highest temples to burn incense to the gods. When presented with the incense, I flatly refused. They insisted I didn't have to pay anything for my incense (which had to be bought), I could use theirs. I tried to explain, as best as I could, that this was not my god, and no incense burning would be happening by my hand, no matter who paid for it.

Back at my hosts' home, I was intrigued by their collection of DVDs, which included, of all things, 'The Ten Commandments'. When I watched it with my host sister, I said 'This is my God!'

In Japan I was strongly conscious of not only being separated from the life I had always known in The Fellowship, but of also being surrounded by a multitude of idols and man-made gods. In response, I sought God fiercely, seeking his presence and reassurance in the midst of foreign faith and superstition. Far removed from anyone I knew, surrounded by a different race and culture, God remained with me, and I conversed with him at length each night. One night as I prayed on my knees, an overpowering presence filled the room. It was sudden and overwhelming, and I froze in fear. I knew without a doubt that this was not the presence of anything associated with an idol god, but a presence somehow associated with the One who is above every 'god' – almighty and awesome. A God who is not to be trifled with. Somehow I felt I was not yet equipped to deal with his presence so directly. Like Moses before the burning bush, I hid my face. I could only whisper 'please, please leave, it is too much'. The presence gently lifted and dissipated.

Despite the little I truly knew about God at this time, I was left without a doubt that he was acknowledging that he knew me. He was hearing me. He was with me.

Journey to the Edge
1993

I know now, Lord, why you utter no answer. You are yourself the answer. Before your face questions die away. What other answer would suffice?

- C.S. Lewis

In March 1993 I began a university degree in Arts, majoring in Japanese language. As my mother had always strongly encouraged me to get a further education, it took me a while to realise that most of my Two-by-Two peers did not attend university, and that it was generally not common among The Friends. That said, it was becoming a little more common among those who lived in the city. Like most things, the unspoken 'rule' depended on where you grew up and what workers you were under at the time. My university attendance was probably an aberration; most of my Two-by-Two friends left school at 16.

As I began my degree, David got an apprenticeship with our Territory's water and electricity board, but then promptly lost it due to the late discovery of his mild colour blindness. This unexpected turn in his path saw him undertake an Associate Diploma of Mechanical Engineering instead, studying at a different tertiary institution.

University became a blessing in a way I could never have imagined. I didn't overly enjoy the classes and barely studied, but I became aware of a Christian group on campus that presented lunchtime sermons twice a week. I was extremely wary, but determined to try to learn more of what other Christians taught and believed. I began to attend, slipping in quietly and avoiding other attendees wherever possible. Fortunately, universities are a great place to blend in and get lost in the crowd. The two weekly sessions had identical sermons, run so that students who missed one due to their class schedule could attend the other. I made a habit of attending both, even though the same message was preached.

The preaching was like nothing I had heard before, working through chapters of the Bible in portions, with every verse expounded in context. The most wonderful thing of all was that I did not have to upset my parents, as they did not know I was attending these gatherings. Whatever rebellions young people may get up to in their university years without their parents' knowledge, this was mine.

There was also a weekly women's Bible study, so I decided to go along to a few of those, despite feeling extremely intimidated at the prospect. Fairly early on, I was invited to a welcome 'get-to-know-you dinner' for female students planning to join a Bible Study. So I decided to attend. No one knew I was going, and I didn't know any of them. I pulled up outside in the dark, and made my way towards the house. Talking and laughing emanated from inside, but also what sounded like rock music. I stood outside for several minutes, seriously contemplating running away and not coming back. I had rarely ever socialised with other adults outside of the Two-by-Twos. We were expected to maintain a distance from all outsiders, a mentality that I continued to find very hard to overcome for years after I left. I had a few school friends who were outsiders, but was quite unpractised in group socialising. And here I was, entering a den of outsiders – 'Christians' of all people! People who went to *false churches* and listened to *doctrines of men and the devil*. Eventually summoning the courage to go in, I found them extremely warm and welcoming. But I was perched precariously on the edge of my comfort zone - me with my waist-length hair and ankle length skirt - gazing at women with short hair, wearing jewellery and trousers, and listening to contemporary Christian music. Stuck awkwardly between worlds, and floundering around like a fish out of water, I was terrified out of my brain.

I was also attending youth group occasionally with David, which met for a youth Bible study every second week, in between social outings. The first Bible study I attended was led by David's older brother. Wanting to include me, he asked me to read a passage from Romans. I flipped around the pages awkwardly.

'Where's Romans?' I finally asked.

Suffice to say there was quite some confusion over the fact that I had supposedly attended some church all my life, but had no idea where to find the book of Romans in the Bible.

As I sat in a university lecture hall one day to listen to the next sermon in the series on Hebrews, the speaker, Dave McDonald, began to preach on the sacrifice of Jesus. He was up to Hebrews, Chapter 9.

Now the first covenant had regulations for worship and also an earthly sanctuary... When everything had been arranged like this, the priests entered regularly into the outer room to carry on their ministry. But only the high priest entered the inner room, and that only once a year, and never without blood, which he offered for himself and for the sins the people had committed in ignorance. The Holy Spirit was showing by this that the way into the Most Holy Place had not yet been disclosed as long as the first tabernacle was still functioning. This is an illustration for the present time, indicating that the gifts and sacrifices being offered were not able to clear the conscience of the worshiper. They are only a matter of food and drink and various ceremonial washings — external regulations applying until the time of the new order. [NIV]

Yes, I knew something about sacrifices being offered for the sins of the people in the Old Testament. They had to try to keep the laws of the covenant, and then offer sacrifices year after year to atone for their sins.

…But when Christ came as high priest of the good things that are now already here he went through the greater and more perfect tabernacle that is not made with human hands, that is to say, is not a part of this creation. He did not enter by means of the blood of goats and calves; but he entered the Most Holy Place once for all by his own blood, thus obtaining eternal redemption. The blood of goats and bulls and the ashes of a heifer sprinkled on those who are ceremonially unclean sanctify them so that they are outwardly clean. How much more, then, will the blood of Christ, who through the eternal Spirit offered himself unblemished to God, cleanse our consciences from acts that lead to death, so that we may serve the living God! [NIV]

Of course Jesus didn't need a sacrifice on his behalf, he was perfect. He had no sin. He showed us the way to live, so that we too, might have a hope of heaven.

…For this reason Christ is the mediator of a new covenant, that those who are called may receive the promised eternal inheritance—now that he has died as a ransom to set them free from the sins committed under the first covenant.

For Christ did not enter a sanctuary made with human hands that was only a copy of the true one; he entered heaven itself, now to appear for us in God's presence. Nor did he enter heaven to offer himself again and again, the way the high priest enters the Most Holy Place every year with blood that is not his own. Otherwise Christ would have had to suffer many times since the creation of the world. But he has appeared once for all at the culmination of the ages to do away with sin by the sacrifice of himself. Just as people are destined to die once, and after that to face judgment, so Christ was sacrificed once to take away the sins of many; and he will appear a second time, not to bear sin, but to bring salvation to those who are waiting for him. [NIV]

The preacher explained that Jesus is the 'once for all' replacement for all of those sacrifices of animals, atoning for our sin not just for a year, but permanently. It was as though a tremendous light suddenly descended through the ceiling as I listened, spellbound. It was all so obvious, and had been in the Bible all along! Why hadn't anyone told me this before? I had sat under preaching - many times a week - for my entire life, and I never knew this? It suddenly all became very clear, and I was exuberant. Although I did not yet realise the implications of accepting this sacrifice as my very own, I finally understood and believed how Jesus' sacrifice could atone for the sins of fallen human beings. His perfection was not to show us how to be perfect, but so he could BE the atoning sacrifice without blemish. He is our Passover lamb, shielding us from eternal death.

Yet despite this epiphany, I couldn't yet connect the dots from this truth to my own faith. How did this truth apply to me? What did I have to do? Was I supposed to be in The Way or was I supposed to leave it? Was The Way just another church? If it was, would it be so bad to leave it for the sake of a different church? Or was this just all a trick of Satan, using a boyfriend to lure me out of God's *'One True Way'* into a *false church*?

This was, in fact, a very real concern. If I left The Way, was I choosing David over God? It was something I continued to wrestle with for a long time. The more I wrestled with it, the more I realised that the storm clouds of an immense spiritual battle were looming on my horizon. This was not simply about choosing one church over another. Something much more serious was at stake. I could feel the tension of forces vying for my very soul.

Six months into my university degree, I got a call from the Australian Government Public Service, offering me a traineeship. The previous year I had undertaken an entrance exam, from which those with the highest results are selected off the top of the list as positions become available. I had just completed my first semester of an Arts degree, but had no real plans as to why I wanted a degree or what I would do with it. I jumped at the chance of immediate admittance into the public service, which provided on-the-job training combined with paid study leave for completing a compulsory certificate in office administration through a tertiary institution. Presented with this opportunity, I left university and entered the workforce as a trainee with the Department of Defence. The earlier twist in David's life subsequently saw him also enter the same department as a trainee technical officer. Soon we were both trainees with the same government department, and then we were working two floors apart in the same building.

My traineeship was a combination of two days study and three days office work each week, for which we were paid a low partial salary. In a class of about twenty, we quickly formed small cliques, and I found myself veered towards Aaron, Katrina and Steven.

How or why we ended up together I don't know, but in that first week I found myself sitting at a luncheon table with them, as we each introduced ourselves and where we came from. Strangely, all three were church attendees from different denominations. I was more than a little perplexed when each of them introduced themselves as a Christian and declared where they went to church. Was this some kind of strange plot? Had I entered the Twilight Zone, whatever that was? I was the last to speak. As they all turned to me expectantly, I knew what they wanted to know. Did I go to church? This was now a little awkward. I tried to explain that yes, I belonged to a group, but we didn't have a name. We had the one true ministry on earth, patterned after the example of when Jesus first sent out his disciples. My response sounded confused, and was followed by a long silence. A few polite questions were finally asked, but I could detect their unspoken conclusions. Weird, closed group. Probably some kind of cult. They did not question any further. The topic was changed as I looked at them all in wonder. We had gravitated together, but I knew nothing about these people. I had never met them before, and yet all three were Christians. What were the chances?

Meanwhile, I was still attempting to strike a precarious balance between The Way and David's church, and pressure was mounting at home. I was still supposed to be attending meetings, praying and giving a testimony every Sunday morning, Sunday night and Wednesday night. For a while our gospel meetings were held on a Sunday afternoon from 5-6pm, after which I would try to rush to David's church for the 6.30pm evening service. This was fraught with many difficulties, not least the resistance of my parents. I was now living in two worlds, and didn't know to which one I belonged. Darkness seemed to have closed in on me so heavily that I felt completely blinded by it, and couldn't see past it to any future.

'Lord, how did I get here?' I cried out often. 'I didn't choose this! I tried to avoid this!'

I would go over and over the past, trying to figure out where I had gone wrong, what I could have done differently to prevent reaching this point. The conclusion was always the same. I hadn't chosen this path – God had. I had done all I could to resist talking to David, but God had insisted. I had been more and more heavily burdened until I had relented. With this conclusion in mind, the only logical answer was that God must have something in mind for the future, and was leading me there through the blackness. At times it seemed so black that I couldn't even see my own hand in front of my face, but had to trust that God did.

As the months of this precarious balancing act wore on, the more frightened I became by what I was doing. Over a period of time, one particular line of reasoning emerged. It began with the introduction of a Church History course being held at David's church on a week night for a period of about eight weeks. As I was still attending The Meetings it was a very painful decision to reach, but I reasoned along the following lines. What I learned would be simply history that had occurred in the world between the time of the New Testament and now. I would not be learning other doctrines, I would simply be learning facts of history, truth. How could there be a danger in that? If I wanted to learn truth, surely this would be a good place to start - by finding out what had really been happening in church history since Christ's time. I was also curious to know if I would find any kind of evidence of an early apostolic Two-by-Two ministry continuing on past Jesus' death. Considering the claims I had grown up with, it had become no small issue. I finally made the decision, and faced my family and the workers, timid but determined.

My parents grieved as they saw me taking one more step towards destroying my faith in the *One True Way*. The workers were furious. I remember explaining it to them very carefully as they sat in my parent's lounge room. I explained that I needed to find truth for myself. They berated me for my foolishness, for following my own wisdom rather than that of God's. They tried to remain calm, but when I refused to concede to them, things turned increasingly sour.

'What are you doing, why do you need to look back into the mouldy pages of history to find truth?' one of them cried. 'We are living here, today, now. Digging up the past is foolish and unwise; why can't you just believe what you have been told, what God has already revealed to us?'

'Would you call the Bible the mouldy pages of history?' I asked. 'The Bible tells us what has happened from the beginning of the world until just after Christ, there have been almost two thousand years since then! I just need to find out for my own sake what has happened in that time. I do not know anything about other Christian churches.'

The workers became increasingly angry, telling me again that I knew the truth; the ministry of the original apostles had continued to where they were today, continuing as the only true and valid form of ministry.

'There is only *one way*' they said repeatedly. Knowing something now about William Irvine, this line of argument did not wash well with me, and in my frustration, I eventually blurted out the forbidden truth.

'Anyway, you know this does not go back to the apostles! This group only started at the end of last century!'

The atmosphere changed immediately, and I could sense a great danger in what I had said. The younger worker jerked in his seat as though he had been struck, and glanced towards his elder companion for a reassurance that did not come. I instantly realized that the younger worker honestly did not know what I was talking about. The older one caught his breath, and avoided looking at his companion. 'We will not discuss this' he declared coldly. The conversation was over.

That following Sunday I sat in the gospel meeting and listened to a very pointed sermon on the evils and pitfalls of trying to unravel the past in our own wisdom.

'Some people,' exclaimed the worker, 'some people believe they can find truth in the mouldy pages of history!'

It was all I could do to restrain myself from standing and hurling my hymn book at him. I admit to spending a few moments indulging gratifying thoughts about what might happen if I did.

It was becoming increasingly obvious to the workers that I was nurturing *a wrong spirit*. Professing members can be referred to as having a spirit preceded by any number of adjectives - a *wrong spirit*, a *questioning spirit*, a *doubting spirit*, a *troubled spirit*. I was showing signs of all of the above. The possibility of being accused of having the wrong type of spirit usually engenders careful compliance with the status quo, as having a *right spirit* is all important. The charge of not having a right spirit, or of having a wrong spirit, is used for control in almost every way, especially pertaining to behaviour, appearance and compliance. It is a charge against which it is very difficult to defend oneself. It is almost impossible to say, with any graciousness and conviction, that you don't have a wrong spirit, when a worker has pronounced otherwise. Your very pronouncement of innocence will condemn you, for even as you answer back, they believe their condemnation is proven. You have asked difficult questions? Not complied with the dress code? Argued a point with a worker? A right spirit will only be restored when full compliance is observed. You are snookered, whichever way you look at it.

I knew I really had only two options here - submit to the workers completely, and restore a right spirit, or start thinking outside the box. The latter would indicate that I had probably reached a point of no return.

My previous conditioning aimed to prevent this. The workers constantly warned against *giving the devil a foothold* to stop us from thinking outside the box instead of conforming and submitting. We were reminded continually that the workers were there for our own good - our spiritual guardians - sacrificing their lives to bring the gospel to us. There is much guilt when considering how much more the workers sacrifice than the average member. The workers had sacrificed for me. How much more did I need to strive to be worthy, considering their sacrifice of home and family?

David was facing his own struggles. At first he had been intrigued by my description of The Way, and attended a number of meetings. He had questioned the workers and questioned his own church. His questioning of his own church had been well received and even encouraged by his minister, and he had come away with a firmer faith, standing on his own spiritual feet for perhaps the first time in his life. He had taken a hammer to both our foundations, and was convinced that only his had withstood the blows. He was satisfied in his own mind, but knew I was far from reconciled to his understanding.

Some of his family were convinced I would not leave The Way, concerned that perhaps I was too brainwashed. He had been counselled a number of times by his brothers to leave me be, because I was unlikely to change. He had a strong burden and prayed urgently. Many times he was not able to say much more than 'Lord, help me!' He said that he always got the same answer: 'Wait.' For more than three years, he was told to wait. Against the counselling of others, and even against what he himself felt was the right thing to do, he was told to wait. At least three times when he resolved to break up with me, he was again told to wait.

At the end of three very long years, he decided there was no hope left, and eventually decided it had to end. But on that very night he planned to tell me, he heard me express something he had not heard from me before – I admitted that perhaps The Way was not the only way after all, and perhaps there were other Christians. It was only the tiniest crack in a huge wall, and yet it was there. He told me years later that he also had a vision that year of me being baptised in his church. He was convinced to hold on and wait – yet again.

David could see how far I had come, but somehow I couldn't take the final steps. He knew I was sitting on the fence, neither fully in The Way, yet not out of it either, and that it was taking its toll.

'You cannot keep sitting on the fence' he said one day. 'You need to choose one option or the other; you cannot stay like this.'

Yes, we were now in love, but we both knew that our relationship had no future if our spiritual differences could not be reconciled. Neither of us really had a compulsion to plan marriage and a future together if we were divided on faith. And yet of course we desperately wanted to be together. Our courtship could be aptly expressed in the words of Dickens, except that ours was the tale of two lovers - *'it was the best of times, it was the worst of times'*. We were deliriously happy spending time together only if we made a concerted effort to ignore the painful reality of our situation.

Despite understanding the true message of the gospel, I had not stepped out and taken hold of it, and therefore remained trapped in a dark room of rapidly staling belief. I had pushed with all my might on the heavy, barricaded door of comprehension, and was mentally and spiritually exhausted. Nevertheless, it had opened a crack, and fresh thought was now flooding in like sea air. It made me almost afraid to breathe, but it was more impossible to shut the door again and stop this invigorating flow. Eventually I pushed the door further and further, and breathed deeper and deeper, but met with the same terrible dilemma that David could already see. One cannot live in a doorway. It is a threshold to be crossed, not a place to settle. One has to go outside, and shut the door behind, beginning a new journey. Or return inside, shut the door, and stay in the place of old familiarity. I was stuck in the doorway, a spiritual agoraphobic.

It became very obvious that something had to be done. The Way door had to be permanently closed, with me on one side or the other. It was too late to just slam the door shut from the inside. I could no longer bear the stale air, now that I had breathed the fresh air. But unlike Alice in Wonderland, who threw herself down the rabbit-hole with little forethought, I pondered long and hard. I didn't want to stare at the inside of a door for the rest of my life. Yet it was too late to walk away from the door and pretend it didn't exist, because I'd already looked through it. Somehow I knew I had already reached a point of no return. Despite these insights, I was still terrified of even *thinking* for myself. Thinking for one's self about spiritual matters was a very dangerous area. It might lead to a *questioning spirit* rather than an obedient spirit, and then the devil might *get a foothold*, digging his toe into your heart and using it as an anchor to claw up into your brain, attacking your mind and faith. My wings of thinking were far from developed, and were atrophied into little flightless, naked stubs. I first had to figure out how to grow some feathers on them, let alone use them.

The reader, having seen my progress so far, may be forgiven for wondering why I simply could not seem to progress beyond this point. But my mental incarceration was still a solid reality. My whole mind was encased in a cage, and as it tried to enlarge to allow new thoughts, the bars of the cage pressed painfully. I was intensely frustrated by this cage and wanted those bars to spring open, but could not find the key. To ease this pressure, I backed off, and considered the issue of thinking itself. Was I allowed - by God - to think? Was it wrong to wonder and ponder and explore thoughts? Did God give me a brain and thinking ability and then say that I couldn't use them? This was a genuine puzzle to me. The answer may seem obvious, but not to those in The Way. We were constantly told we had to be *as little children*, which meant accepting whatever we were told by the workers, who acted as our authoritative, all-wise spiritual parents. We were exhorted to have a *soft heart*, which meant one that was completely pliable to the will of the workers.

My mother had been fighting this same battle for years, as she admitted to me late one night in a moment of weakness. There were so many things she didn't agree with, so many things she wanted to question. She often wondered if The Way was the best thing in her life, or the worst thing in her life. Was it the cause of her deepest moments of unhappiness, or the glue that held things together? There were certainly times when she wished that her parents had brought her up in a 'normal' church, where being a Christian meant having a real concern for others, ministering to those in prison, caring for the needy. She poured out many concerns and woes to me that night. The next day she retreated in fear, worried that she would push me further from The Way rather than keeping me in it. It wasn't really that bad, she assured me. She had just indulged in a moment of weakness and said things she ought not to have. I wondered who she was really trying to convince – me or herself. In hindsight I realise she had long sought to put doubts aside because of the unbearable psychological pressure of living in a state of uncertainty over the foundations of her own faith.

One day an interesting thought occurred to me as I paced up and down the fence line of my thought boundaries. What did Jesus say about thinking? Did he want people to think for themselves about what he said? I immediately turned to the Bible and a concordance. I had asked David for one as a gift for my birthday, and he eagerly responded with an enormous Exhaustive Concordance (for some reason the workers have often discouraged concordances). In this instance, it was invaluable. As I turned to the word 'think', I was taken by complete surprise to discover that one of Jesus' regular phrases was 'What do you think?' He asked this question continually of his hearers and disciples as he spoke with them. He seemed to be repeatedly exhorting them to switch on their minds and really consider his words, not just take them at face value. I felt a surge of new hope. Jesus did not oppose me thinking for myself! He *wanted* me to think! I had at last found the key to the cage, and started turning it, slowly and cautiously.

Mentally, I had been checking out of The Meetings for some time, although I had continued faithfully attending meetings and professing. When I had last attended convention, I knew in my heart it would be the last. The spell was broken. It felt like an out-of-body experience - watching everyone go through the motions of convention like actors on a stage, while I stood at a distance like a silent and unseen audience. These were no longer my people, and I no longer felt any affinity with them. The strings had somehow been cut, and I was no longer dancing to the tune.

The final leap came in the form of a Sunday morning confrontation with my parents. I would not be attending the meeting in our home that day. I was leaving the house early, and would instead go to David's church. I told my mother as calmly as possible, but the ticking bomb finally triggered, and emotional devastation erupted. She was sure that my father would have a heart attack and die due to my decision, and it would be my fault. When it became clear that I could not be moved from my resolution by any means, my father was summoned.

'You do know this is the only Way, don't you?' he asked gently.

'No Dad, I really don't' I replied. 'This is why I have to go and find out for myself.' It was a significant moment, and we all knew it. At that instant, I had stopped professing. I wasn't attending meeting. I was heading off to a *false church*.

It was time to cross the threshold, and close the door firmly behind me. I did. Like Alice, I didn't know where all this would lead, but in the end I had little option. I finally decided to hurl myself down the proverbial rabbit-hole. And, like Alice, I suddenly found myself falling down a very great, deep blackness.

Condemned

You have put me in the lowest pit, in the darkest depths.
Your wrath lies heavily on me;
you have overwhelmed me with all your waves.

- Psalm 88:6-7 [NIV]

In the week that followed, the blackness became far deeper than I could ever have imagined. The first thing to overwhelm me was utter fear, triggered by the workers' regular warnings that those who leave will have something terrible happen to them. My mother was beside herself with fear and grief over my decision, and warned me repeatedly that something dreadful had been revealed to her. A strong sense of foreboding pervaded every moment, until I could no longer bear to be at home. As the first days went by and there appeared no chance of me changing my mind, Mum told me, in sheer desperation, what she had seen when she had opened her Bible a few days before. She didn't want to tell me, but was certain that it was a warning not to listen to me.

If your very own brother, or your son or daughter, or the wife you love, or your closest friend secretly entices you, saying, 'Let us go and worship other gods' (gods that neither you nor your ancestors have known, gods of the peoples around you, whether near or far, from one end of the land to the other), do not yield to them or listen to them. Show them no pity. Do not spare them or shield them. You must certainly put them to death. Your hand must be the first in putting them to death, and then the hands of all the people. Stone them to death, because they tried to turn you away from the LORD your God... (Deut. 13:6-10) [NIV]

My insides clenched into a tight knot, and stayed in a constant state of severe contraction that wouldn't release. Those first few weeks I suffered unrelenting and awful abdominal pain. The next few months were enveloped in a kind of fog. I began to suffer more and varied physical and emotional symptoms of significant stress, frequently becoming agitated and shaking all over uncontrollably.

The strain of living at home became too great, especially as I was required to keep setting up the meeting room, and any possible ruse would be used to prevent me from getting out of the house on Sunday morning before The Friends arrived. Sometimes I would be too late to get the car out of the driveway, and would have to escape out the back door, and walk the two kilometres to David's church. But I was granted some merciful relief in the form of several housesitting offers. So I left home, albeit temporarily, and tried to recover my mental and physical equilibrium.

Instead of feeling relief, I fell into a state of deeper and more dreadful terror. With the foundations of my former faith stripped away and nothing left to stand on, God allowed me to see myself as I stood before him, and my heart melted in fear. Despite trying to be a good professing girl belonging to the one true church, I knew my heart was full of wickedness and deceit, impure motives of every kind. God revealed to me that my sins were detestable in his sight, and I could never stand before him, no matter how 'good' I tried to be. I wanted to run and hide, to have the mountains cover me. There was a black, bottomless pit within my own heart which I could not escape. I even briefly understood why some people might contemplate suicide, but that seemed the worst option of all, coming under the judgement of an awesome God even sooner. I encountered a righteous and holy God, and knew I could never measure up, no matter how hard I tried. Wearing my hair in a bun certainly would not improve any moral standing. Nobody taught me this, or preached this at me. It was more like seeing my reflection for the first time in a real mirror instead of rippled, muddy water.

I could not stomach food, suffering nausea and the constant abdominal pain. I lost a great deal of weight and my hair began to fall out again (I had suffered a severe case of measles a year previously; with hair loss triggered by the sustained fever). I had great trouble holding down my job. My physical problems, combined with my now very fragile state of mental health caused a lot of difficulties at work where I was in training as a public service officer in finance, as I could not concentrate on anything. My supervisor was very concerned, and when he found me curled up under his desk one day, took me to talk to the director. My supervisor and director had realised for some time that something was very wrong, and urged me to see a doctor. I did end up seeing a doctor who gave me time off work. I was suffering anxiety and Post Traumatic Stress Disorder, although I did not know it by that name for several more years. I didn't know what was wrong with me, except for the obvious spiritual and emotional turmoil.

One of the most difficult aspects of my condition was the sudden, involuntary panic attacks that occurred regularly, at the most inopportune times. I might have been riding on a bus, walking in a shopping mall, watching a film, sitting at home having dinner. They seemed to be preceded by – nothing. I could not determine any trigger. I could not prevent them. One minute I would be having a good day, my mind preoccupied with various mundane things, and the next I was reduced to a quivering mess with no warning. I wanted to shout at my body and pound myself in frustration. What? What is your problem? What caused it this time?

There was no answer.

There was no safe place.

I couldn't prevent them.

I couldn't stop them.

I was physically, mentally and psychologically helpless against myself.

I felt desperately alone at this time. I could not explain my torment to others, and I did not know anyone who had left The Fellowship and still walked with God. David was my best friend and confidante, but I couldn't adequately explain what I was going through. I was theologically illiterate and spiritually bankrupt, flailing around trying to find a solid anchor point. Distrustful of spiritual leaders, who had proven to be deceitful to their very foundations, distrustful even of myself in a body that seemed to have reeled mentally and physically out of control, what or whom could I trust?

I resumed work, but I was completely consumed with a hopeless despair. I knew how I appeared before God, and there could be no salvation for me. Sitting at my work desk one day, I could bear it no longer. I picked up the phone and called David's minister, asking if I could see him that day. I left work that same hour to see him, not really knowing why, or what I would say, but I was completely at the end of myself and did not know where else to go.

When I entered Pastor Bosker's house, I was so overwhelmed I just sat and cried for some time before I could speak. I haltingly tried to express my confusion and inadequacies, and begged repeatedly 'What do I have to do to be saved?'

A Telephone Directory

'Twas grace that taught my heart to fear,
'twas grace my fears relieved
How precious did that grace appear,
the hour I first believed

- John Newton, Amazing Grace (lyrics)

What did I have to do to be saved? To the Rev Bill Bosker, the answer was obvious.

'Oh Elizabeth, you don't have to do anything to be saved!' he cried. 'Jesus has already done it for you!'

I didn't understand at all. The last piece of the puzzle was missing, and I simply couldn't find it.

'I think we need a telephone directory' said Bill. And off he went to get one. He came back and placed both my palms facing upwards. He waved the heavy telephone directory before me.

'Let's say that this book contains all of your sins. Not just everything you've already done, but everything in your life – past, present and future. A complete record of all you've ever done and will ever do against God.'

He indicated my left hand, palm up. 'This hand represents you. Between you and God is …' he placed the directory over my palm '…the complete record of your sins against him. There is no perfect fellowship with God because you are separated from him by your sins. When he looks down on you, this is what he sees.'

Then he indicated my right hand, palm up.

'This hand represents Jesus. Sinless, in perfect fellowship with God. When God looks down on Christ, there is nothing separating them, no sin dividing them.

Now, when Jesus died on the cross, he took upon himself all of your sin.'

At this point the telephone directory was transferred from my left hand to my right.

'If you believe on the Lord Jesus Christ, all of your sins are on him. He takes the burden of them, and the penalty for them. When God looks on Christ, that is where he now sees your sins. But when he looks upon you, there is now no record of sin.'

I looked at my empty, left palm. There was now nothing between me and God. No record of sins.

Bill opened up the Bible and read from Ephesians 2:8-9, which were quickly to become my favourite verses of the Bible: *'For it is by grace you have been saved, through faith—and this is not from yourselves, it is the gift of God— not by works, so that no one can boast.' [NIV]*

Bill also explained that if any religious leaders insist that we have to keep all sorts of rules in order to be right with God, then they are laying heavy burdens on men, as warned in the Bible. He spoke about the passage in Luke 11:43-46,

'Woe to you Pharisees, because you love the most important seats in the synagogues and respectful greetings in the marketplaces. 'Woe to you, because you are like unmarked graves, which people walk over without knowing it.' One of the experts in the law answered him, 'Teacher, when you say these things, you insult us also.' Jesus replied, 'And you experts in the law, woe to you, because you load people down with burdens they can hardly carry, and you yourselves will not lift one finger to help them. [NIV]

I thought of the workers eating at a separate special table at convention. I thought of them sitting in reserved seats in the front row of the meeting shed. Separate accommodation, separate food, separate seating and separate treatment. I thought of the workers going from house to house, checking which rules were being broken. The workers had often inferred that ministers from *false churches* of the world were the Pharisees of our day. For the first time, I could clearly see that the description instead fitted the workers almost perfectly.

Like Christian in Pilgrim's Progress, I had finally come to the foot of the cross myself, and my heavy burden had rolled off. It was very surprising to me too, that the sight of the cross should thus ease me of my burden. As I made my way home that day, I felt like leaping for joy. I had not read Pilgrim's Progress at that time, nor did I have any idea what the story was about. When I shared my joy with others, someone remarked 'You sound just like Christian at the cross!' They were right. I later read it and found his song of joy:

> *'Thus far I did come laden with my sin;*
> *Nor could aught ease the grief that I was in*
> *Till I came hither: What a place is this!*
> *Must here be the beginning of my bliss?*
> *Must here the burden fall from off my back?*
> *Must here the strings that bound it to me crack?*
> *Blest cross! blest sepulchre! blest rather be*
> *The Man that there was put to shame for me!'*

- Christian, in John Bunyan's 'Pilgrim's Progress'

Physical freedom must be very difficult to adapt to when one has been incarcerated for an extended period of time. I had been mentally incarcerated for many years, and this new spiritual and mental freedom needed some adjustment. Despite my new understanding and rejoicing, my life did not change completely overnight. Although my fear abated substantially, it was still there. It was a fear I didn't want to give voice to, but I couldn't shake the remnant of doubt that perhaps I was wrong. Perhaps the Two-by-Twos were the only right way, and I had taken a wrong turn. It was a constant nagging in the dark recesses of my mind that continued to bring on anxiety and panic attacks. Why wasn't I healed of all this emotional trauma and spiritual doubt? I expected everything to be miraculously better overnight, but it wasn't.

Over time, I learned that God is not into magic wands or Band-Aids. We humans are incredibly complex, and our creator God is not simplistic in his healing. Where we want instant solutions, he wants spiritual growth. He doesn't wipe the slate clean of all spiritual, mental and physical traumas that we experience as part of our human condition. We have to work through it, like everybody else. We need to continue to learn what it is to be a human, and struggle with the same struggles as our unbelieving neighbours. If God dissolved every problem we had whenever we asked for it, we would be the most uncompassionate, self-righteous and arrogant beings on the face of the earth. Instead, we realise more than ever our need of him, and seek his grace in facing our daily struggles. We come to learn that he is the one who we need most, and the one who can never be taken away from us, in life or in death.

God did not immediately take away my troubles. Instead, he provided great comfort and assurance by continuing to show me his hand in some miraculous ways. He continued to confirm that - despite my doubting - he was still leading.

A Mental Institution

A bruised reed he will not break,
and a smouldering wick he will not snuff out.

- Isaiah 42:3 [NIV]

Some months after leaving The Meetings, and after a number of housesitting stints which came my way, I felt that I really needed to leave home permanently. I was welcome to stay there as long as I wanted, but I needed some space to establish my new faith. As I was now working full-time, it was financially feasible, so I moved into an apartment with a girl from the church youth group.

I was now free to attend the local church (the Reformed Church of Canberra) along with David and his family. I was also able to start a private Bible Study with a Christian friend from youth group, to start catching up on some theological understanding, sorely lacking in my life to this point.

One Sunday at an evening worship service in late 1993, the pastor was praying. He prayed for a lady not known to the congregation, 'Nerida' (not her real name) whose acquaintance with someone from the church seemed fairly obscure, but for whom he had been asked to pray. Nerida had just been admitted to the psychiatric ward at the local hospital. As he said her name, a voice spoke in my mind.

'You must go to visit her – tomorrow night.'

That voice again. I was surprised and confused and far from thrilled at the prospect. I had no idea who this woman was. Why would I visit her? What would I say?

The voice was strong and insistent, and laid a heavy burden on me.

The burden became heavier and heavier the next day, and I could think of little else. I thought of every excuse possible and tried to discount this urge as being completely irrational, but I had a growing sense of unease which forced me outside and into my car that next evening. I had not visited this place before, and had only a vague idea where it was. I set off towards the psychiatric unit at the hospital. It started to rain, and then pour. Then came the thunder and lightning and wind. I drove down the main road towards the hospital with minimal visibility, peering through sheets of water on the windscreen.

'What on earth am I doing?' I muttered to myself. 'I must be crazy. I think *I* need admitting to the psyche ward. If God really wanted me to go, surely he would have given me safer driving conditions.'

I found my way there and buzzed the intercom on the outside of the building. I introduced myself as a visitor, and the security door released to let me in. I was a bit surprised. I could have been anybody gaining admittance. Wait – I was just anybody. Was this really normal procedure? A nurse enquired whom I was there to see.

'Um, Nerida?'

'Sure, I'll call her room, and she should be right down.'

This presented a bit of a problem. Not only did I not know Nerida, I had no idea what she looked like. And she didn't know who I was. If Nerida walked down the hall, how would I know it was her? And how would she know I was her visitor? I felt like I was watching a movie and on the edge of my seat waiting to see what would happen next. Stranger arrives at a psyche ward on dark and stormy night to confront a mentally ill patient because a voice told her to. Really, Lord? Maybe I *had* lost the plot. I was starting to feel like a complete fool.

A woman walked down the hall towards me. She walked right up to me and said 'It's you!'

'Yes, it's me' I said. And I recognised her, too.

Fortunately this is a true story. Because I've heard that the difference between writing truth and fiction is that fiction has to make sense and be believable. Not even I could believe what was happening right now.

For the past few years, I had been working in a small corner grocery store several nights a week and all day every Saturday. This woman, in her sixties, had been a fairly regular customer. Only I didn't like her. I was annoyed by her extreme slowness and hesitancy about everything, and was often impatient while serving her. She often came to the shop with her elderly mother, who was bossy and intimidating towards her daughter. I knew this woman well by sight, but had never known her name.

And now here we were, face to face, recognising each other immediately under the strangest of circumstances. We went to the ward's lounge where we sat down and made small talk for a few minutes.

'I'm planning to commit suicide tonight' announced Nerida suddenly. Now things were becoming truly intriguing. Whilst most people might have no idea what to say to this, I knew exactly what to say. I had just completed a study component where we had to do a research paper and class presentation on a subject of choice. I had chosen the topic of suicide, and had spent the past six months researching it. It was a subject close to my heart because both my piano music teacher and a classmate had committed suicide within the previous few years. I now knew why I was here.

I asked her what she was planning and exactly when. This is important to determine the exact nature of the disclosure – is it a cry for help, or seeking attention, or is the plan well underway and close to being finalised?

Hers appeared close to being finalised, and yet she had told me (a sign of seeking intervention). Whether or not she could have carried it through to completion while in psychiatric care, I don't know. But I also didn't want to have it tested.

I asked her to enter into a contract with me - that she would promise not to commit suicide, and I would promise to come back and see her. After much hesitancy and conversation back and forth, she finally - albeit reluctantly - agreed.

After a while she said 'Why did you come here?'

'God brought me here' I said simply.

We were both quiet for a moment, and her eyes filled with tears. 'He knew what I was going to do.'

Mine filled with tears too. 'Yes, but he sent me to see you.'

I went back to see Nerida the next day. She was so excited to see me.

'I kept my promise!' Her eyes shone. 'I said I would, and I did!'

I saw Nerida a few more times, but we did not keep in touch much after that day. Occasionally I would see her at a distance walking on the street, but then I heard she moved out of town. I don't know what her journey has continued to be, but I was so humbled to be able to share a tiny part of it by God's hand.

I feel the need to add a disclaimer here about 'signs' and 'messages' from God. I have never sought nor asked for signs from God. The only words that we may truly know are from God and trust in completely are those we find in the Scriptures. This has to be the case, otherwise we would constantly be bombarded on every side by people claiming to have new 'revelation' from God. On what basis could we trust any of these revelations?

I had, however, been born into a system where I was conditioned to view the Scriptures through the interpretation of the workers. I had been further conditioned not to question their teachings. Sometimes it may take extraordinary intervention by God to counteract those who have acted in his name, and break us out of bondage. He may choose to use strange and sometimes mysterious ways to do it.

There have been very few occasions in my life when I have heard a voice speak to me, all but one of which I have already shared. In these instances of hearing a voice, I'd like to point out a couple of things. I was not expecting it, nor asking for it. I was extremely cautious; I did not presume that they were 'messages from God'. I do not in any way advocate seeking or trusting in messages we may feel we have been given - we could be wrong. We must test all things to see if they are from God, and the only fully reliable source of truth from God is his Word, the Bible. Ultimately, we only know if something is the work of God through the fruit it produces when it comes to completion.

I did not tell anyone of these instances of 'hearing a voice' for some years, not even David. I never used them to declare 'God has revealed this to me...'

These were intensely private and personal dealings, and I didn't feel comfortable sharing them with anyone.

While I believe that God chose to communicate with me in some astonishing ways, I still do not believe that God would want anything he laid on my heart to be used to manipulate other people into doing anything supposedly for him. It is all too easy to say 'God told me ...' and use it as a justification for insisting that others must therefore believe or do what we say. God has created us as intelligent and rational beings, and he demands no less from us than our full application of these faculties in our examination of the scriptures and walk of faith with him.

Take note that even the Scriptures can be abused. For example, purposely relying on chance by opening the Scriptures at random to receive a 'message from God' upon which to act in a certain circumstance is akin to gambling – taking a valuable resource and wasting it in a foolish game where we stand to lose more than we gain.

The very few instances of hearing a voice speak to me each occurred during the time of God revealing himself to me, leading up to and culminating in my public profession of faith and baptism as a Christian, after which I have not heard the voice in that same way again. God seemed to use some extraordinary means to break through the spiritual bondage in which I was snared. I praise God that the Holy Spirit was able to lead me into all truth, to come to know Christ for myself.

So now I bring you to the last instance that occurred during this period. One night as I prayed, kneeling at the side of my bed, I was interrupted by a voice that spoke to me.

'You need to be baptised'. I was mid-sentence in prayer when this interruption occurred, and I was again quite startled by it. I hadn't given any thought to baptism, for reasons that will become clearer in the next chapter. But this time I didn't resist and I wasn't sceptical. I understood the plan of salvation. I had believed, and now trusted in Jesus as my Lord and Saviour. I immediately saw that the only thing I had failed to do was to express this publicly.

So that week I asked David to accompany me to see the Reverend Bill Bosker. He and his wife were excited to see us, but Inneke stayed in the kitchen while we spoke to Bill, and I put my request to him. Eventually he called in his wife to share the good news. She, however, couldn't quite hide her disappointment. 'Oh, I thought you were going to announce your engagement!' she cried.

My request to make a profession of faith and be baptised was put to the church's Session - a council made up of the minister, elders and deacons - which oversees the running and pastoral care of the church. I was to attend the session meeting myself, to explain my understanding of faith to them, and answer any questions they put to me. The elder personally assigned to provide support to me at the time seemed to be trying to prepare me carefully for this meeting, but I wasn't in the least concerned. I looked forward to this meeting with much anticipation, as I finally knew and understood the gospel. I didn't realise until later that some of the elders viewed me with some scepticism. Was I joining the church because I was in a romantic relationship with David? Was this a marriage-seeking conversion? I appeared before them completely oblivious to this aspect. Some confessed to me later what had been in their mind, but after hearing my proclamation of faith, they felt somewhat ashamed of having suspected ulterior motives.

I understood their concern, but it was the last thing on my mind. I had struggled with the opposite problem – I hadn't wanted to join the church until I was completely sure that I wasn't doing this just for David. David and I were not yet married, or even engaged. I still had no real guarantee that we ever would be. I had to be fully responsible for my own actions. Whatever I did now would set my future course with God, regardless of whether or not David and I had any future together. But I was now sure beyond any doubt that Jesus was my personal Saviour.

The Anti-Christ

In the beginning was the Word, and the Word was with God,
and the Word was God. He was with God in the beginning.

- John 1:1-2 [NIV]

With the decision made to be baptised, and my new understanding of the gospel, my thoughts turned again to the Two-by-Twos.

Professing, also known as *making your choice*, is a completely separate event from baptism in The Way. You must prove yourself for up to several years of professing, showing that you have the *right spirit* and are obedient and *worthy enough* to be baptised. Baptism may then be granted, or withheld until certain further conditions are met. Or other privileges may be withheld until one is baptised; some couples may not be allowed to marry, even if both are professing. Conditions placed on baptism can be extremely arbitrary, depending on the worker in the area at the time, and how worthy or submissive the applicant is deemed to be.

I had professed for nearly 3 years, from 16 to 19 years of age. And I was a late starter. Most of my peers had well and truly been baptised by the time I was 19 and still unbaptised. Yet, I just couldn't bring myself to request it. I refused to do anything for the sake of appearances, and God had certainly not laid it on my heart to be baptised. So I had waited.

Obviously it was now a relief both to them and to me that I had not been baptised by the workers, given my apostasy against Two-by-Two doctrine and departure from The Way.

Since I had stopped going to meetings, none of the workers had contacted me. I simply disappeared, and they did not seek to follow up with me.

I had come a long way since my last interaction with them. I now knew what I believed - with certainty. I understood that Jesus was in fact God, the Word made flesh (John 1). I understood that he was the complete sacrifice for our sins, and that his righteousness was the only righteousness that we could ever have merited to us. It bothered me enormously that the workers didn't seem to understand this. Perhaps they had never heard the true gospel. Someone had to tell them! I felt strongly compelled to share this message with them, desperately wanting them, too, to be freed from spiritual bondage to their own good works which could only ever be as filthy rags in God's sight (Isaiah 64:6).

I contacted the two workers who were in Canberra at the time. It was now March 1995, and in the period of time since I had left, different workers had come to the area. They happened to be the overseer of NSW, along with a much younger companion - only a year or two out *in the work*. I found out where they were staying, contacted them and asked to see them. They were not overjoyed. In fact they were extremely reluctant to meet with me, which was quite bizarre. What true shepherd, having a member of his flock disappear, would not follow them up? Despite their constant preaching to the contrary, there was no sign of them going after the lost sheep.

I can only surmise that workers usually prefer meeting with people on their own terms. They usually request the meeting and set the agenda. They are very uncomfortable discussing spiritual matters where there is direct questioning of their beliefs. They prefer to verbalise their doctrines in gospel meetings to captive audiences, or to followers who know better than to contradict them or ask difficult questions.

Nevertheless, I finally managed to persuade them to meet with me. I drove to the other side of the city to the home of a married couple where they were both staying. They had managed to arrange for me to enter and leave without being seen by the owners of the house; whether by design or not, I do not know.

I told them how my understanding of the gospel had changed, that it was not our own efforts that merited anything, but the work of Christ. On this basis, I now believed we could have full assurance of salvation. The older worker told me I was arrogant and presumptuous to think this way. I asked him about Paul the apostle, and the total assurance he seemed to have in his faith and eternal destination – why couldn't we have that same assurance? Surely Paul the apostle was just a mere human being like us. It seemed far beyond their scope to accept that I could compare myself with someone from the Bible. I tried another angle.

'If you were given the chance to ask Paul why he had this assurance, and on what basis he expected to be let into heaven, what do you think he would say?' I asked.

The older worker considered this for a moment.

'He would say, "because I have done my best"'.

'No, he would not.' I said. 'He would say, "because I am trusting in Jesus' blood"'.

I tried my best to explain the Bible's teaching that Jesus is actually God. This got their attention.

'This is of the antichrist' declared the older worker. 'If you believe this, you are the antichrist.' He opened to 1 John 2 and read from verses 22-23:

'Who is the liar? It is whoever denies that Jesus is the Christ. Such a person is the antichrist - denying the Father and the Son. No one who denies the Son has the Father; whoever acknowledges the Son has the Father also.' [KJV]

He seemed to believe that I was 'denying the Father and the Son'; ie denying that they were separate persons by calling them both God. But the passage is actually talking about those who deny that Jesus is the Christ - by implication they are denying the true identity of the Father and the Son.

I tried to use some other verses to show the deity of Christ. I opened to Hebrews and read chapter 1, verses 8-10:

But about the Son he [God] says,

'Your throne, O God, will last for ever and ever; a sceptre of justice will be the sceptre of your kingdom. You have loved righteousness and hated wickedness;

therefore God, your God, has set you above your companions by anointing you with the oil of joy.'

He also says,

'In the beginning, Lord, you laid the foundations of the earth, and the heavens are the work of your hands. [NIV]

To my surprise, the younger worker started laughing mockingly.

'Why are you laughing at me reading this?' I asked, bewildered.

'That's just a clever New International Version translation' he sneered.

I was truly stunned. I had not realised they did not accept anything except the King James Version as a genuine translation of the scriptures.

'What does your Bible say in this passage?' I asked.

He opened to the passage, but refused to read. Three times I asked, but he still wouldn't read it.

'It depends on how you translate the word 'God' here' he said finally.

'I don't think God calls anyone God except himself' I replied.

The older worker had had enough.

'Elizabeth, we're very sorry that this has happened to you.' he said. 'But in a couple of years, you'll be back. This sometimes happens, but in the end you'll be back. In the meantime, I want you to go home and pray that God will open your blind eyes.'

'Would you be willing to pray that same prayer?' I asked.

Of course he would pray no such prayer; it was appalling that I would dare to say such a thing to any worker, let alone the overseer of the state. He shook his head and continued to repeat his request for me to pray to God to have my blind eyes opened.

'I'm very sorry, but he already has' I replied firmly.

'Well, I hope you're happy now' was his only parting remark, to which I responded by looking at him squarely.

'Happy is a very shallow word' I replied. 'I'm much more than that. Maybe peace, contentment or joy is a much better description.'

I left, very disheartened, but also astounded. Their knowledge of the scriptures appeared extremely limited, far more than I imagined. I knew my own knowledge was still fairly woeful, but had assumed the workers would have had some better knowledge than just demonstrated.

I was baptised in the Reformed Church of Canberra on 25 June 1995. My parents were invited but declined. On the 11th of July 1995 David and I were engaged, to be married early that coming December.

Our impending wedding presented a variety of challenges. I had a huge extended family on both sides, all of whom were members of the Two-by-Twos. There were also others of The Fellowship - long term friends - my parents wanted to invite. David and I, and his family, were part of a separate church family with many members. And this was before we started to count in other personal friends from school or work.

There was also the difficulty of the ceremony itself. Weddings in The Fellowship usually consist of the exchange of vows only, presided over by a civil celebrant in a neutral venue (usually a garden). Being married in a church building, by a minister of religion, would be a highly controversial issue for my family and relatives. For some unexplained reason, brides in The Way were not permitted to wear bridal veils. It is only in more recent times that they have even begun to wear bridal gowns; previous generations had worn a serviceable street dress.

David could not entertain the thought of being married by a civil celebrant rather than our own minister. It was also the custom at our church for weddings to be conducted in a worship service. And finally, he thought it appropriate that his bride be permitted to wear a veil, as she was no longer subject to the legalisms of The Way. We decided that the venue and form of the ceremony should belong to us. It seemed important that our marriage reflect our personal faith, not impinged upon by restrictions and beliefs of the Two-by-Two system. It would be entirely inappropriate to hold a Two-by-Two style wedding when we both belonged to another church. My parents could make the decisions regarding the reception.

In the end, family and closest friends had to take priority, along with just a handful of friends from The Fellowship on one side and my new church family on the other. We had a morning wedding, followed by a morning tea at a chapel in the city and official reception at lunchtime, formally held by my parents.

We then went on to our own chapel in the evening, where an informal 'reception' was held by our own church family - everyone brought a plate and we enjoyed a casual evening meal and time of fellowship together.

After nearly five years of tumultuous courtship, a controversial wedding ceremony and two receptions, we were finally married - on my own parents' 24th wedding anniversary - on Saturday, 2 December 1995.

The Fullness of Freedom
1995

But when 'grace and truth were realized through Jesus Christ,' a long-awaited revolution of the heart began to set religious captives free. Fear-full bondage motivated by guilt was replaced with a fresh motivation to follow Him in truth simply out of deep devotion and delight. Rather than focusing on the accomplishments of the flesh, He spoke of the heart. Instead of demanding that the sinner fulfil a long list of requirements, he emphasized faith, if only the size of a mustard seed. The change spelled freedom, as the Lord himself taught, '...you shall know the truth, and the truth shall make you free' (John 8:32). Rigid, barren religion was, at last, replaced by a grace-orientated, relationship-liberating grace. His followers loved it. His enemies hated it... and Him. Without a doubt, the earliest grace killers were the Pharisees.

In the first year of our marriage, David and I went out to dinner at a local Chinese restaurant. The same restaurant, in fact, that both our families had frequented over the years as we both grew up. Not overly surprising, given that we grew up in houses less than 2 kilometres apart.

'Do you think we were ever both here together on the same night with our families and didn't know it?' I mused this particular night.

'I don't know' said David. 'But I was here once with my family the same night as two whole tables full of girls – boy, did they make a lot of noise.'

'I was here once with two whole tables of girls' I responded.

'It was someone's birthday' he reminisced. 'And I know there was someone called Louise there.'

'It was someone's birthday when I was here with all the girls' I recalled, 'and there were actually two Louises in our group'.

'A girl with long brown hair kept staring at me.' Dave looked at me and I laughed.

'Yeah, sure. Wait … that was you!' I had a moment of sudden and total recall. 'You kept looking at me! You were sitting with your family in the middle of the room, and you were on the end of the table. You kept looking at me!'

'Only because you kept looking at me!' he protested.

'I remember my friend asking me why I was so distracted that night'.

'Yeah, I remember Mum asking me what I kept looking at, and when she saw all the girls, asked me "which one?"'

'How old would we have been?'

'We must have been 14 or 15.'

We both sat there completely dumbfounded. We had seen each other before. Several years before we actually met, we'd laid eyes on each other across a room and something had taken hold of us. And neither of us had remembered it since, until we'd both sat in the exact same place together, years later. We were again in awe at the mysteries of life, and the workings of a Sovereign God.

I had now had so many confirmations of the hand of God at work in my life in the past few years, and yet I was still adjusting to my spiritual and mental freedom. That remnant of fear was still holding on by a persistent and very stubborn thread. It was most disconcerting; why was I still troubled?

One night we went out to a dinner party with some former classmates of David's from high school. Over dinner the subject of my past came up, and I sought to explain something about the group I had grown up in and come out from. Those present had never heard of this nameless church before.

'Hey, have you thought about looking them up on the internet?' asked one guy.

Actually, I hadn't. This was the mid-1990s, and the internet was only just becoming widely used. We didn't yet have it at home, and had only just been connected to it at work. I was excited at the prospect. Would there be anything on the internet? I searched as soon as I got a chance, and very quickly came across a lot of information about the history, identical to that already revealed in The Secret Sect. There were others out there exposing this stuff! I fired off an email to one of these websites created by someone based in the United States, explaining that I had come out of the Two-by-Twos and was now a Christian.

The next day was a watershed for me. I received a response from Joan Daniel, and what a response it was. It revealed that not only was she also a Christian, but she was part of a much wider forum of many others who also knew the same truths of the Gospel which I had discovered, and all had their own personal stories of their painful exits out of the Two-by-Twos.

I had finally reached the core of what had continued to trouble me. I had known no one else who had come out of the group and had a personal confession of faith in Christ. While I had stood completely alone in this, I continued to experience fear. If I was the only one, wasn't it possible that I was wrong? Otherwise there would surely be others. Maybe I had just been influenced by David and his 'false' church.

Here, finally, was a deep sense of vindication. I was not the only one. Others, many others, had come to the same conclusions and made the same discoveries as I had, independently. They now professed the same faith I did, even though they were on the other side of the world, and attended many different churches in different denominations. There was one faith, one hope in Christ, and we had all been brought to it. They rejoiced to find me, and I leapt for joy to find them. Not only that, but as I read their stories, I came to a much clearer understanding of the fear and trauma that had overwhelmed me. Many others had also suffered post trauma stress. I hadn't been going crazy. I had been undergoing a normal human reaction to the strain I'd been under. The relief was immense, and the last vestiges of doubt were swept away by this tidal wave of confirmation which had swept across the oceans from the other side of the world via the internet.

These were great days of discovery and communication and debate as many of us chatted incessantly over the internet on a forum, investigating the similarities and differences of what we had each experienced. But I was also very naive, not stopping to consider that many other silent 'lurkers' were creeping onto the forum, watching and listening from the sidelines, including workers who knew me. I perhaps could have been more discreet, but in the end hope that their presence benefited them more than it harmed me.

I was one of the first people from Australia to make contact with the ex-members in America via the internet, and readily agreed to become a point of sale for books about the Two-by-Twos for Australian customers. This was before the days when consumers regularly made purchases of merchandise overseas via the internet; having an Australian distributor would make it much easier and cheaper for people to purchase the books. Joan sent me a small package with *Reflections* and *Reflected Truth* so that I didn't have to wait several months for the first shipment of books to arrive. I devoured them in about two days, and think I barely slept in that time. These were the collected, short memoirs of many individuals who had come out of The Way, with all of their varied experiences and treatment at the hands of this very human and very faulty system.

Several days later I was standing in the kitchen of our small rental home. All of a sudden I had an amazing sensation of two enormous wings rising up either side of me. It was as though two wings I never knew I had suddenly lengthened and spanned the room. I could feel power and strength surging through them, and could move them back and forth. I felt an incredible peace and joy flow through me, radiating from the centre of my being, right through to the tips of my wings. I had a deep sense of being completely free, and now able to soar. All chains of spiritual bondage had finally broken away, and I stretched outwards with all my might. It was an amazing moment, one I have not shared with anyone until the writing of this book almost 20 years later.

I now had an array of books and pamphlets about the Two-by-Twos in my possession. What exactly would I do with them? I made some firm decisions early on. I would always be upfront about what I was doing. No deceit, ever. I would not send information to anyone unsolicited - those who received this information would have to be mentally ready for it, and want it. I would not act anonymously. I would tell people who I was, where I was, how to contact me, and what I was distributing. I had no intention of hiding what I was doing or being secretive in any way.

My first action was to telephone the current workers in the area and ask to see them. I took the bull by the horns, but initially the bull wouldn't budge. It took an enormous amount of coaxing to get them to agree to see me. When they finally did, it was under an extraordinarily strict agreement. They would only see me if I agreed not to tell anyone they had been to see me. I was not to reveal their identities, or repeat what they said to me to anyone. If I ever told anyone they had visited me, or if I ever repeated anything they said, they would publicly deny it.

Their request was bizarre, and completely without integrity. They were seeking, in advance, to absolve themselves of lying, should I ever reveal their visit or repeat what they said. They were, therefore, obviously unwilling to stand by anything they said. They were also willing to publicly (and falsely) denounce me as a liar, and politely warned me in advance that they would do so if I didn't play by their agenda and rules. Why? Was this senior worker and his younger companion really that frightened of me, a twenty-one year old? Again, why? I sought only to tell the truth, and seek the truth. It was becoming abundantly clear that their modus operandi was deception and lies.

I agreed not to reveal their identities or the conversation that took place that day. I did present them each with a packet of books and pamphlets. I told them what I was doing, and that I would be giving the information to anyone who asked for it. I told them I had been lied to and deceived about the history of the group, and they had both an opportunity and responsibility to tell the truth themselves before people found out by other means. I asked them to read the materials I gave them, and tell me if they found any error, lies or slander therein.

Without going into detail, suffice to say they expressed that it was no longer any of my business, as I had now left. I begged to differ - it was completely my business. I was one of the people who had been deceived by them. They showed no interest or remorse whatsoever that others would continue to be deceived, repeating only that it was no longer my concern.

I am still not interested in exposing who these men were, because it was never my intention to trap them or trick them for ulterior motives. I always intended this to be a private meeting and a private conversation, for the purpose of sharing with them literature I had, and appealing to them to stop the deceit over the origins of the group. I still held some naive belief that truth would mean something to these men. I was appealing in vain. They indicated that they would tell whatever lies it took to keep me silent.

While I don't regret having met with them, I did unwittingly provide them with quite a bit of ammunition against me, the backlash of which became apparent almost immediately. As I was to find out, it made no difference if I kept my end of the bargain. I was publicly branded a liar and enemy of their fellowship anyway. Nevertheless, what man intends for evil, God is able to work for good.

I discovered the immediate consequences of my actions when I received my first hate mail.

Anonymous, of course, sent both to the post office box I had rented for the purpose of Two-by-Two correspondence, and to my home address; the implication being slightly menacing – 'we know where you live'. And then anonymous emails, full of spiteful name calling and abuse. I had nothing but contempt for this form of communication. At least I was able to respond to emails, if not to postal mail. My message was straightforward – If you have something to say to me, say it without the name-calling. If you disagree with me, let's sit down together and discuss it reasonably. And if you have any courage at all, step out and identify yourself. Only cowards hide in the dark and lob stones over the wall. I didn't hear from such people a second time.

I did hear from someone who was willing to identify himself. He contacted me via email, upset because he claimed his family formerly had a convention ground on their property 'going back several generations' and he insisted that our claims of the history of the Two-by-Twos was wrong. He believed that the convention grounds predated the William Irvine founding date shown on internet sites about the Two-by-Twos. I responded that we would take his issue very seriously, and were only interested in discovering truth. I asked him to please investigate further, and see what evidence he could find to support his claims. To give him every credit, he did get back to me a little while later to report that his investigations proved he had been wrong. Still, he supported The Way and wanted to continue in it.

I have had many phone calls, emails and letters from people over the years, mostly in association with them purchasing books about the Two-by-Twos. Many of the messages have been very kind and thankful notes of support. Someone even obtained and sent me an original copy of William Irvine's death certificate from Jerusalem; it obviously meant enough to this person to carry out their own research about the historical claims made in *The Secret Sect* book about the life and death of William Irvine. The receipt of this certificate seemed a nod of vindication to me that I was telling the truth, no matter what others said or were told.

One night I got a very strange phone call. A couple, whom I did not know, called to ask who I was and what I had done, because they had been severely warned by the workers not to contact me. A very interesting conversation ensued, in which I learned that I had been publicly denounced, by name, by the workers. The Friends were warned about how dangerous I was, and that no one was to contact me or have anything to do with me. For some, it apparently had the opposite effect - they contacted me to ask what this was all about. As usual, the workers had spoken in riddles, not giving any clear indication of what I was supposed to have done, but had instead given me an air of intrigue and danger.

Another gentleman who phoned me was still very committed to The Way, but was also interested in hearing about who I was and what I had done, and what I was now doing, spiritually. I explained to him my discovery of who Christ is, and that I now attended another church.

'Well, I'm very glad you have found another way' he said.

'No, that is not it at all!' I replied. 'It is not "another way", it is Christ himself. Where I go to church is not the primary concern. There are any number of churches I could attend; my faith is not dependent on a particular church.'

He was uncomprehending, and kept referring to 'another way' that I had found, much to my frustration.

My discoveries and activities as a now former member were rudely interrupted one day when I was informed by my family that the older of my two younger brothers had requested to be baptised. Both of my brothers had professed after I left. My family was very keen for me to attend the baptism. There is an almost superstitious belief among The Friends that if a former member can just be enticed back into their presence, *the spirit* may be able to grab hold of them again. I wasn't keen to attend, although not for such superstitious reasons. I honestly couldn't be happy that my brother was being baptised by this group which did not believe or preach the true gospel of Christ. However, family is family and I went, and David came along to support me.

Most of The Friends were polite but kept their distance. Only one literally and purposely turned his back on me. I have few recollections of the day, but do remember that I had a brief encounter with a senior worker, and wrote about it on an online forum. A few days later he phoned me, furious about what I had written. It was my first real indication of how closely they were watching everything I did. I realised for the first time that they had probably been privy to everything I had written for the past few months. Not that it greatly concerned me, as I didn't feel I had anything to hide. But this was the one and only time a worker ever contacted me voluntarily after I left, and I didn't want this opportunity to go to waste, especially as this was also a worker I had provided with a package of books and pamphlets.

'Hey, since you're calling, could you tell me what you thought of those pamphlets I gave you?' I asked. 'Was there anything false or slanderous in them?'

He grudgingly admitted there was not, and that they seemed to be a fairly accurate representation of his group.

'However,' he continued 'we obviously have a different understanding of the gospel.' He was referring to a particular pamphlet section which compared the 'gospel' of the Two-by-Twos with the gospel of mainstream Christianity.

'We sure do.' I replied.

One of the stranger aspects of leaving the Two-by-Twos was that no-one else from my former life ever contacted me. A whole lifetime of friends, acquaintances and fellow meeting attendees saw me disappear from view and never sought interaction. If you leave, they really do prefer not to hear from you again. To me this was unsatisfactory. I had real friends - or thought I did - those I grew up with, had spent countless hours with, had numerous sleepovers with. Did I really not even exist to them anymore? I continued trying to contact them and visit them. I wasn't trying to stir up trouble - I didn't take books or pamphlets or try to tell them about William Irvine. I just treated them as I always had; they were my friends.

I noticed a significantly strong pattern emerging. I could contact them, but they would not reciprocate. They would often acquiesce to my request to visit them, but were unlikely to visit me. Eventually things came to a head when I made plans to visit and stay with one of my closest childhood friends. I made the mistake of mentioning the impending visit to a relative, and a day or so later the arrangements for the visit were withdrawn via telephone. I was perplexed and upset. Had I done or said anything to offend her? She seemed unable or unwilling to communicate to me the reasons. I was eventually referred to her husband, who laid out the amended 'rules' for any visit I still wished to make. I could come, but not stay overnight. I could have a short daytime visit, but only if I agreed 'not to mention the name of Jesus' in their house. Perplexity turned to incredulity. People who called themselves *God's only true people on earth* would only accept me in their house if I understood that any topic pertaining to Jesus was forbidden?

After this phone call, I became increasingly suspicious. It seemed all too much of a coincidence that my visit had been tampered with after I had mentioned it to a certain relative of mine. I telephoned him, and asked him, point blank, if he had been involved in any way in communication with my friend over my intended visit. He denied it.

I contacted my friend again to make alternative arrangements for the visit. I still wanted to see her, despite its meaning I would have to travel there and back in a day (she lived several hours drive away). I also asked her if the reason why I could no longer stay there was due to intervention by someone. She finally admitted that she and her husband had been warned against me, but wouldn't elaborate. She would not divulge by whom, but I told her it was pretty obvious, as there was only one other person who knew about my visit. She couldn't bring herself to lie when I asked her bluntly if it was the relative to whom I had spoken.

It was. As this relative was an older male and former worker in The Way, I knew that they felt compelled to comply.

Yet again I was being confronted with the true nature of this group. From every angle, it demonstrated cult-like characteristics, quickly withdrawing and closing ranks on me as soon as I was no longer on the inside, issuing vague but strong warnings against association with me, the substance of which was never fully divulged. Deception had again come to the fore. I was furious about this meddling in my long-term private friendships, but the writing was on the wall. With deep sadness I knew that any such friendships could only be continued on a superficial level, and only if I trod very carefully and agreed to meet on their terms.

I went ahead and visited my friend. I also confronted my relative and had a few strong words to say about the situation - first for interfering, then for lying about it. The Way might operate in deceit, manipulation and control of its members, but I was no longer willing to let it go unnoticed. I would call them on it.

Very soon my mother would be forced to call them on it, too.

False Conviction
1996 - 1997

*The important thing is never to give power over an individual
to a person who doesn't have to answer for his actions.*

- Sir Roy Douglas Wright

My parents, of course, were still regularly and faithfully attending all of the meetings, but I did give them a copy of the book *Reflections*. Initially it sat untouched in their house, but curiosity eventually got the better of my mother. She started reading, and was astounded to recognise her own reflection swimming to the surface of the pages. Questions and doubts, long weighed down by obedience and compliance, started to rise again. It may have been easier to dismiss these stories if there had not been a name and address after every account. These were real people, with real experiences, and many of them sounded just like her.

She began taking the NIV Bible to meetings rather than the commonly accepted (old) King James Version. She began taking her Bible with her to gospel meetings to check the content of the verses mentioned, and the relevance in what was being preached. She began to evaluate the message spoken – was it good and right and edifying? Sometimes it sounded right at the time, but then, on the trip home, she was surprised by how quickly problems surfaced with what she had just heard. Concerns began to develop in how useful the 'sermons' were for application in everyday life. Were these practical messages, to direct and guide and help and change lives? To show sin for what it was? With a growing awareness of sexual misconduct by the workers and accusations of paedophilia against some, she was no longer willing to quench questions and doubts. She was beginning to feel like a pot plant that was badly root bound.

Mum became less guarded in her comments and questions to The Friends and workers, enough to raise eyebrows and become a growing cause for alarm. Several visits by the workers ensued and my mother, causing further unease, asked some difficult questions.

Mum had another reason to be particularly upset at this time. My parents had been assisting in the care of a young cousin of mine. He had *professed* in The Fellowship while living with them in Canberra. He later went to live with another aunt & uncle further north, but was stopped from taking part in the meetings by the workers in that location. He had committed a minor offence of mischievousness after a gospel meeting one night, and was stopped from professing on the grounds that he might be a *bad influence* on other young people. This appeared to be the extent of their 'pastoral care' - excommunication for a minor misdemeanour - when we now knew that far more serious sins, even by the workers, were being swept under the carpet.

Injustice, misconduct and deceit all suddenly seemed to be compounding. Rather than retreating, she advanced further in her questioning. Why were the origins of The Fellowship not openly talked about? Why was it such a big secret? Why did the workers not want to talk about salvation by grace? Before long, the workers called and said they were coming over for another visit. They rang one morning, and told her they would be coming for lunch. Mum hurriedly prepared a special meal, including a pavlova for dessert, and rang

Dad at work to request he come home. It is likely that they arranged a midday visit in order to meet with her alone, but Dad made arrangements to come home from work.

The workers didn't waste much time getting to the point. Alarming reports had reached them. In addition to the divisive issues she had already been raising, she now stood accused of discussing divorce with someone - querying the doctrine which forbade remarrying under any circumstances.

There was also a more serious charge - she was accused of influencing new converts against The Way. A couple of young Croatian men - outsiders - had been coming to gospel meetings and had been impressed with what they saw. Mum, being particularly friendly with strangers, had probably had a conversation with them at some point. She was now accused of having given them unauthorised pamphlets about The Way. Mum had no idea what the workers were talking about. This charge against her was completely untrue - she had not given anything to new converts, in fact she did not even have any of the pamphlets in her possession, nor had she even seen them. The workers knew I did, however, and Mum's *questioning spirit* had caused them to assume that she herself had the pamphlets and was distributing them. They put two and two together and came up with five.

But her denials were irrelevant. They pronounced judgement quickly, with no discernible evidence. She was having her *part taken away* from her, effective immediately, unless or until all of her 'understanding' fell into line with the understanding of the state's workers. This meant she could no longer speak or pray in The Meetings. She could not take the bread and wine. She would still be permitted to attend meetings, but had to be completely silent. Her silence would indicate a severe censure from the workers, the cause of which she would not be permitted to explain. It is the equivalent of an excommunication, and their intent was unmistakable. This sudden turn of events was completely unexpected. Mum rose up from the table where they were seated.

'You're wicked!' she exclaimed. She repeated it again before leaving the room in great distress. The workers remained seated in silence for a few moments, before rising, gathering themselves and quickly departing. The pavlova remained untouched.

The senior worker who excommunicated my mother later had a discussion with the Croatians about 'those pamphlets you were given by Cherrie'. The young men asked what he meant; they had not received pamphlets from anyone. Who was Cherrie? They may have met her at the meeting, but couldn't even be certain who she was. The worker should have been badly shaken. Here was solid proof that he had gotten it wrong - very wrong. His bluff had been called. Instead of retracting his accusations, however, he decided to tamper with the evidence. He confided in the young men that this was a 'private conversation', and should remain so, 'lest it cause difficulty or upset to anyone'.

In God's providence, Mum actually bumped into these young men at a local shopping mall a short time later. She recognised them from the gospel meetings, and stopped to talk. When she introduced herself, they immediately recognised the name, and told her they had been asked about some pamphlets she had supposedly given them, of which they had no knowledge. A fascinating conversation ensued, in which Mum became privy to the conversation the worker had had with them. She was made very aware that the worker now knew for certain that she was not guilty as accused. With this knowledge, surely he had a heavy obligation to right this wrong, and at the very least apologise. No such approach was ever attempted. He did not speak to her again. The workers are always right - even when they are undeniably, irrefutably wrong. It is also interesting that these pamphlets were used as a reason to excommunicate my mother - these same pamphlets that this same worker had explicitly admitted to me were a correct representation of the group and its beliefs. Why then, the anger that new converts might have seen them?

At the time Mum was put out of The Way, the worker's words to her were revealing - she heard her own words of recent days echoing in her ears, an indication that she had been informed on by acquaintances with whom she had shared concerns and questions. It was akin to the tactics of the Stasi, East Germany's notorious secret police. Mum's so-called friends had quickly cleansed themselves of her questioning spirit by handing her over to their spiritual authorities. A report against her had been followed by the workers' arrival on her doorstep for swift retribution as a warning to others.

Whereas I had eventually jumped from The Way, Mum had been pushed. She was still a fair way from the edge when they pushed her, and initially went into free fall. While the landing may have been cushioned somewhat by the resources she now had at her disposal, she still experienced grief and rage at the injustice of the events which had unfolded.

Despite her questions, Mum had been still loyal to The Way. She would not have considered leaving, even though she was starting to raise some concerns for which she sought genuine answers. The heart of a matter had always been more important to her than outward appearances, and she never considered she would be pushed if she looked more closely at that which seemed inconsistent. Now friends had betrayed her. The workers had lied in their accusations against her. She was given no right of reply or any chance of arbitration. Judge without jury was her lot. She certainly wasn't going to leave her executed spirit in the midst of The Friends to be gazed upon and whispered about.

The blindfold had been cut off, abruptly and crudely. So much was suddenly exposed that she had no option but to leave. She would not, under any circumstances, debase herself by attending The Meetings and remaining silent, indicating she was guilty of something. From that very day, she never went back to another meeting.

Further insult would be added to injury. Friends from interstate, on hearing what had occurred, later questioned the senior worker concerned. This worker denied that Mum had ever been stopped from *taking part*. His comments were a direct contradiction of events, and made Mum out to be a liar. If Dad had not come home for the workers' visit that day, there would not have been a witness to their duplicity. Furthermore, if she had NOT been stopped from taking part, this senior worker would now have been alerted to the fact that there had been a serious misunderstanding, one that needed correcting. Needless to say, neither he nor any other worker ever contacted her about the situation.

Dad was still an elder, and the meeting remained in their home, a state of affairs which was to continue for another 6 years. Why this is the case is hard to say. Why would a man with an apostate daughter and excommunicated wife be allowed to continue to be an elder and have the meeting in his home? I can only surmise that it was either to reward him for his faithfulness in continuing in The Way despite so much alleged opposition from his own family, or to ensure that it would be much harder for him to leave himself. Or even, perhaps, the workers' unspoken recognition that they had treated his wife atrociously.

Where my mother wears her heart on her sleeve, my father is the opposite, a river where currents run deep while remaining undetected on the surface. Although his long held convictions and deep loyalties kept him bound for the present, this was the beginning of the end for him, too.

Mum, meanwhile, was left as a sudden outcast with no spiritual home. And yet she also recognised that a door had been unexpectedly opened for her by God. A parched soul with far more questions than answers, she read the Bible even more voraciously, spurred on by the revelations of other former members in the book I had given her. Her Bible reading reached epic proportions. She would start first thing in the morning. She would read on throughout the day, and when Dad came home from work in the evening, she would oft times still be reading and unable to stop. As he came in the door he would be bombarded with her discoveries from that day. Did he know the Bible says this? And this? Despite having read the Bible her whole life, it seemed to her a completely new book. She got herself a new Bible, from which she could read afresh, unhindered by the memories associated with the old one. I had done the same.

Released from her own mental incarceration, she read and questioned everything. Now she could ask the questions openly, without fear of condemnation or reprisals. But who to ask? She experienced similar struggles to what I had, not being particularly trusting of anyone. She mostly worked through the Bible for herself, recording lengthy notes about her investigations, discoveries and ongoing questions.

'It is actually quite exhausting' she remarked to me one day 'having to sort everything out for yourself. There are so many churches out there, how do you know which ones are right?'

This is a problem commonly faced by those exiting a cult. No matter what difficulties there may be inside, it has defined boundaries and rules. Stepping outside the boundary, or being pushed out, is often overwhelming. Where are the new boundaries? Who will tell me what is right and what is wrong? Whom do I trust? It presents quite a dilemma, particularly if you have been taught all your life that no one on the outside is to be trusted and that churches, especially, will lead you astray with their doctrines from the devil. The greatest temptation is to look for another 'way' - another system to replace the one you've found to be faulty. As prisoners released from incarceration are suddenly overwhelmed by the lack of enforced routine and the huge number of decisions they now have to make, so former cult members often initially struggle to discern anything for themselves.

All of these things take significant mental adjustment. On leaving the Two-by-Twos, I continued to look like one for nearly 3 years. I wore the same clothes, and had the same hairstyle. Partly staying in my comfort zone, and partly not wanting to frighten my family by looking too different, too quickly. As I walked along a sidewalk one day, I caught sight of my reflection in a shop window, and thought one of The Friends was behind me. As I turned, I realised it was my own reflection. At that moment I decided to start changing my appearance. It was another realisation of just how deeply I had been conditioned, and how hard it was to step out of my old life.

The Exodus
1995-2002

*Sometimes what you're most afraid of doing
is the very thing that will set you free.*

- Robert Tew

Not wanting to stay in the house on Sunday mornings whilst the meeting was in progress there, Mum started coming to church with David and myself almost immediately. Word did seep about among some of The Friends concerning how Mum had been put out of The Meetings, and she received messages of support. A few wanted to have her reinstated by appealing to workers with higher authority, but after short consideration she realised she wasn't interested. She was now out, and had a clear view of the workers, unhindered by blind compliance. As she surveyed the scene from afar, she knew she never wanted to go back.

With the use of internet becoming more and more common and widespread, information about the Two-by-Twos was exploding across the globe. There were many former members in the United States and United Kingdom lifting the lid on their experiences. People who exited could now post 'exit letters' online for all to read. A newsletter for former members called *Forward Press* was started in the United States. We became aware that there had been a mass excommunication in Alberta, Canada, referred to as the 'Alberta issue', although no further clarification or information was available for some time. Initially, no one seemed willing to expose what had happened, perhaps because the wounds were still so raw, or those dis-fellowshipped still held out hope of being re-admitted.

This would only be possible if they continued to demonstrate complete loyalty to The Way.

Here in Australia there was an exodus of families in Sydney in the mid-90s, and then also in Mildura. We all conversed freely and exchanged notes online. Soon we were attending conventions together again - this time we converged at a multi-denominational annual Christian convention in Katoomba, New South Wales. It was a very different experience to our former conventions. This time we came from different churches in different denominations. We rented our own holiday houses and were free to come and go as we pleased from the convention grounds, and meet with whomever we wanted. In the midday breaks, we would congregate for a lengthy lunch followed by cheese and wine late into the afternoon as we discussed faith and theology. We talked about the former days and rejoiced in our freedom. For more than ten years, many of us met together every year at this convention, our own form of group therapy. It wasn't just ex-friends, though. The wider group was made up of many other Christians from our home congregations who put up with our idiosyncrasies and cheered us on in our newfound freedom.

It was into this environment that my father finally ventured, slowly and cautiously. Fully convinced that he would never cross the threshold of my church, I was proven wrong when he made an appearance with my mother at a Good Friday Easter service in the late 90s. He couldn't attend on Sundays, as he was still the elder at the meeting in his own house. He did, however, start attending the annual Katoomba conventions with us, held in the Blue Mountains just outside Sydney. It became a running joke among the ex-friends that he still hadn't left The Way, and they made sure to jovially ask him and rib him about it each year. Dad's attendance at these conventions while still an elder in the Two-by-Twos remained one of the best kept secrets among the ex-friends for some years.

Closer to home at around this time, an evening public talk was advertised on the subject of the Trinity, to be held on campus at the Australian National University. Seeking to get a stronger grip on their understanding of this doctrine, my parents were keen to come along with David and me. We found our way into the correct building, a lecture hall with multi-level tiered seating. We got ourselves comfortably seated and watched as other arrivals filtered in and filled the rows. One of us suddenly noticed the unexpected arrival of two familiar figures - male workers. As we all turned around in surprise, they couldn't help but see us too. They acknowledged us as minimally as possible and took their seats at a distance. Afterwards, we noticed that they departed as quickly as possible through the furthest exit from us. It was quite evident that they did not, under any circumstances, want to risk engaging in a conversation with us about the topic of the talk. They had spotted my father there, of course, listening to *false doctrines of men* while still an elder, but what could be said about that? They couldn't very well raise the topic of his attendance without also acknowledging and explaining their own. Nothing was ever said.

New Beginnings

When she transformed into a butterfly, the caterpillars spoke not
of her beauty, but of her weirdness. They wanted her to change back
into what she always had been.
But she had wings.

- Dean Jackson, used by permission

Sometimes I still cannot quite comprehend that I left The Fellowship. In the earlier years of my life I never conceived of a time when I might no longer be one of them. Because it was, and remains, the cornerstone of my spiritual heritage on both sides to several generations, it is almost embedded in my DNA. Only those of us who have been there know exactly what it is to have been bred as one of The Friends, the product of someone's grandiose spiritual experiment from an era past. Once it was our only reality, but now the memories linger mostly as a surreal dream, from which we awakened to emerge into the rest of the world, fearful and uncertain.

The Friends, having restricted their own world to a small and narrow place, refer often to *those out there in the world*, as though referring to a far-flung galaxy where life is alien and inhospitable. Life is not to be embraced and lived in its fullness in Christ to the glory of God, but to be endured from the confines of their narrowed spiritual observances, peering out through the curtains of their man-made rules and regulations to tut-tut at the appearance and behaviour of their fellow creatures.

I recently watched 'The Shunning', a fictional film about a young Amish teenager - Kate - who finds out that she lives among the Amish as an adopted daughter, not a biological member of the group. It raises significant questions for her, particularly as the Amish do perpetuate almost exclusively through regeneration within their own. To know that her biological parents are out there in the world is profoundly conflicting - was she ever really meant to be Amish?

As a former Two-by-Two, I feel a strong affinity with the Amish. I understand what it is like to look and feel different from the outside world. To be restricted in life opportunities because of expectations. To walk down the street and feel a deep division between yourself and every other person because they *are of the world*.

In 'The Shunning', a particular scene resonates especially deeply. Kate purchases herself 'worldly' clothes, and walks down the street 'disguised' as a non-Amish person. She no longer stands out; nobody stops and stares at her. She is suddenly invisible and anonymous. Even the Amish pass her by without a second glance, because she suddenly holds no meaning for them. Every curiosity, every preconception about her identity and beliefs, has been completely erased, simply by changing her clothes and letting down her hair.

Occasionally I see a group of The Friends at a park or in a shopping centre, and I know in that moment that I am Kate in disguise - invisible and anonymous. I know so much about them, but they will not even see me. They will pass me by without a second glance, knowing that I am not one of them, but one of those worldly people.

Another group which bears a more striking resemblance to The Fellowship is the Exclusive

Brethren. The only external variation is that the Exclusive Brethren women wear headscarves. Whenever I encounter members of this group in public, I am probably a little more fascinated than the average person. I can't help taking stock of their appearance and noting which ones are more conservative and which ones are pushing the boundaries. The 'head-coverings' on some have been depleted to a mere ribbon of questionably narrow width, and I have to smile, knowing that the wearer is barely scraping by with the slimmest imaginable compliance to the head-covering rule. These days many of the women are observed to add a decorative piece to the side of their head band - confections of soft fabrics, lace, net, beads - a nod to fashion and individuality within the limitations of their own parallel existence.

When I encounter them in public I long to say something to them, but I don't know what. To let them know that I understand everything about why they live and dress as they do, but it doesn't have to be this way. But I would be an unwelcome intruder, a worldly outsider, putting dangerous thoughts into their heads. The mothers would quickly take their children by the shoulders and steer them away from me. So I just watch from a distance, knowing that the majority of those children will also grow up never conceiving of a time when they might not belong to the faith of their forefathers.

I find some amusement in the appearance of groups such as the Exclusive Brethren because I know that my own past was no different. We pushed the boundaries of wearing denim skirts to stonewash and acid wash denim (this was the eighties!). I pushed the boundaries as far as a stonewash denim jacket, and then - horror of horrors - a stonewash leather jacket. This last item was an 18th birthday present, but it took some persuading of my parents. My father remained very nervous about this particular piece of clothing. A few weeks after my birthday, I was wearing my beloved jacket when I was spotted in the city by a worker, although I didn't know it at the time. Fortunately, this worker considered my jacket very attractive and feminine, and made a point of informing my father that the jacket I wore was appropriate - so much nicer than most of the leather jackets he had seen. Phew, official stamp of approval granted.

When you grow up with countless rules, expectations and inconsistencies, they become almost natural. But as David viewed the same inconsistencies with fresh eyes, he found them killingly funny. And as I adjusted to the ramifications of the life-changing decisions I had made in leaving, I also started to see the funny side of my former life.

The workers take a skewed interpretation to the scriptural verse *"God that made the world and all things therein, seeing that he is Lord of heaven and earth, dwelleth not in temples made with hands"* (Acts 17:24; KJV), claiming that this is the reason they do not construct or own church buildings. They also condemn any church that does, but meanwhile build big barns in cow paddocks in which to hold their convention meetings - church buildings in disguise (built, presumably, by human hands). Consequently, certain farmers of a certain strange religious group acquire the biggest barns and farm machinery sheds ever seen.

Two-by-Twos may not own televisions, but getting a video card so that recorded films or television stations can be watched via the computer is completely different, according to some of The Friends, because a computer isn't purpose-built to be a television. With the increasingly widespread use of the internet, it eventually became apparent that most homes would be online, with access to far worse (and unregulated, uncensored) material than ever available on television. The resultant situation is that many workers are now online via their personal laptops and smart phones while still forbidding The Friends from having television sets.

David was intrigued when we went to a Two-by-Two wedding. The workers left early, as they often do, to make a public point of indicating that all celebrations should be as short and simple as humanly possible, and that nothing should be celebrated too long, especially weddings (second best to *going into the work*). As soon as they departed, video cameras suddenly popped out of people's bags and festivities were recorded.

'How on earth are they going to watch what they've recorded?' whispered David in my ear with a cheeky grin, knowing that televisions were forbidden.

Another time we were visiting the home of some of The Friends and David was relaxing in the lounge room while I chatted with the wife in the kitchen. A tall cupboard with double doors stood against one wall, and David noticed something strange shining out of the doors, which were ajar. Moving closer, he realised there was a complete television and stereo set-up in the cupboard. Whilst he was making this discovery, the husband of the house entered the room, no doubt also noticing the coloured lights shining forth from the cupboard. When we entered the room later with the hosts, David noted that the doors had been closed and locked.

I admit we have shared many funny stories with other former members of the group about 'the bad old days'. Someone told us about the worker who was nicknamed 'Snapper' because of his propensity to patrol the car parks at conventions, snapping off radio antennas. No chance of escaping to the car to listen to the cricket score, and no point in complaining to anyone about the vandalism to your vehicle – only worldly people followed sports or listened to radios.

My favourite story comes from some overseas acquaintances whose friends had been visited by the workers. During the course of the visit, not-so-subtle comments began to be made about *keeping in step with the spirit*, *having the right spirit*, and *not letting the world into the home*. When there was no appropriate response from the hosts, the rhetoric grew stronger. The poor bewildered friends eventually had to confess they were at a loss in recognising their shortcomings in this instance. The worker went into the kitchen and pointed at the source of their sin - a new microwave oven which he had mistaken for a television set.

That was the lighter side. There were far more serious things I began to hear about – an adulterous relationship between one of the workers and a local wife. Revelations of sexual abuse against children by workers and other members of The Way. Some cases were highly publicised and eventually prosecuted; many more remain shrouded in a cloak of silence. Even for those who have left, the price to pay for revealing their past abuse seems too high, and too traumatic. Many former members who were victims still have parents and siblings in The Fellowship, and exposing their own past sexual abuse would likely cause permanent alienation from extended family where relationships are already under serious strain. Having read *Reflections* and *Reflected Truth*, I realised that the local exposures were nothing new. These problems were occurring the world over in The Way. Experience proved that the heaviest condemnation would fall on those who tried to speak out against the abuses, for bringing The Fellowship into disrepute.

I had an opportunity, in about 2000/2001, to spend some quality time with my next sibling - Anthony – at my grandparents' place, where we were both staying for a few days. We had rarely seen each other since I had left home and married. During that time Anthony had professed in the Two-by-Twos, been baptised, left The Meetings, and subsequently struggled with some dark times in his life. These dark times were not the result of having left The Meetings; rather he had realised that The Meetings could not fill the deep void in his soul.

At one point he made an effort to return to The Meetings, and attended convention with a renewed sense of effort and hope. He saw one of the head workers he had known for many years while growing up, and approached him eagerly, greeting him cheerfully like a long lost brother and thrusting out his hand for the expected handshake. The worker just stared at him and did not take the hand offered.

'What's this scrawl?' he growled before turning away to re-engage in a conversation with someone else. My brother was left with what I can only imagine was a similar shame and fury as I had experienced a few years earlier at convention with the sister worker. His too, was a minor appearance defect - he had grown a small goatee. For both of us, these were the lasting memories we had of our standing in The Way, and the attitude of the workers towards us. Their only priority was what we looked like on the outside; there was no genuine concern or pastoral care of our spiritual struggles on the inside.

Now, however, we had both left, and I was able to tell him of all that I had discovered over the past few years. The truth of the history. The exposures of adultery and sexual abuse. As the night moved on into the late hours, and then the early hours, I was finally able to share the gospel with him, using the same analogy of the telephone directory. The puzzle pieces fell into place, and Anthony suddenly saw and understood the gospel in its entirety. He was overwhelmed. We both cried.

The next day was Sunday, and he accompanied me to a local church in the town where my grandparents lived. Although not the denomination I attended at home, I had been there before and knew they were a faithful local church which preached the gospel. When the service was over, the people in the pew in front of us turned around to say hello and introduce themselves.

'I only found out last night what it means to be a Christian!' Anthony announced to them excitedly. He too, saw the Bible with new eyes, and was suddenly hungry for so much more.

At that point in time, Anthony had been living with a sense of emptiness; in spiritual darkness and bereft of hope. It has been a long journey of spiritual growth since then, and 10 years later he, along with his wife Georgie, made a profession of faith in our church, and presented their three daughters for baptism. They made this profession of faith on my 38th birthday. We can have confidence that once God has brought someone to life through the Spirit, he will carry that work through to completion. We are weak, but he upholds us in his mighty hand. We are powerless to save ourselves, but he is powerful to save.

Purged by Fire
2002-2003

You can tell whether a church is a false church or not if it was started by a man or woman. We are the only church on earth that was started by Christ.

- Jack Carroll, US worker (www.thelyingtruth.info)

In August 2002, my paternal grandmother died. It had been a long and arduous journey in The Way for her. As a young, single woman she had come into contact with the workers for the first time - brought along to The Meetings by a work acquaintance - and *made her choice* to commit her life to The Way. This decision put her at enmity with her own family, as she left their church to join this strange group. While she went on to marry and bring up nine children in The Way, controversy and divisions plagued life among The Friends in the state of Victoria, bringing great turmoil to her own household. To understand something of this controversy, it is useful to go back to what we now call the Early Days.

The earliest formal coalescing of Two-by-Two workers into a recognised separate group, as a sect, appears to have taken place at their first major gathering - Rathmolyon Convention - in 1903, where around 70 converts met for three weeks, and resolved, under the headship of founder William Irvine, to sell and give up all possessions to the common purse. This wholehearted devotion appeared to be a spiritual revolution of sorts against the established church, and an antidote to its perceived lukewarmness. In 1902, Irvine and fellow founder Edward Cooney had begun to gather together converts into Sunday morning meetings, whereas previously converts would have returned to the existing local churches with their respective ordained clergy. These separated gatherings of adherents seem to have constituted the first 'saints' or 'friends' of the workers, although this concept was at first strenuously opposed by Irvine, who would have preferred every 'saint' to forsake all and go out preaching. Workers, having sacrificed home and possessions 'for the sake of the gospel', were inevitably elevated in status above 'friends'. An inevitable Orwellian outcome soon saw workers firmly lodged as the ruling clergy in a two-tiered system; all people in The Way were equal, but some were more equal than others.

In the earliest days of the Two-by-Twos, the Carroll brothers - John and William - from the British Isles were among the most prominent workers. John (Jack) and William (Bill) eventually gained infamy within the group, both rising to the position of Overseer in their respective countries of ministry. In 1904, Jack headed off to help pioneer the work in North America (later becoming Overseer of the Western States), while Bill and his wife Margaret (Maggie) travelled to Australia in 1913 as workers with a daughter, May (Bill later becoming Overseer of the State of Victoria, where my grandparents lived). Workers do not marry these days, but some of the earliest workers were already married when they joined The Way, as were Bill and Maggie. Some did marry after joining the work, but it set a controversial precedent. As it was believed 'true preachers' had to be itinerant and could own nothing but a few meagre possessions, this was highly incompatible with marriage and family. As time went on, workers who sought permission to marry were granted or denied permission on an individual basis, until eventually all requests were denied, or those who did marry had to cease preaching. In Early Days, married workers were often separated and sent out apart; their children left behind for *the sake of the gospel*. Jack Carroll, despite having a married brother worker (Bill), and later blessing the marriage of his worker cousin to a woman who was also a worker, nevertheless later prohibited marriages between workers.

Over in Australia, Bill Carroll's health suffered in later years, and he lived at least his last 10 years in a beach house reportedly owned by his daughter May and her husband, on the southern coast of the state of Victoria, with a boat moored outside. Carroll was in the rare position of having been a married worker with an offspring to provide such support and housing for his later years. Each year at least one male worker and one or two female workers were assigned to Carroll as his servants in lieu of going out to preach. Many of The Friends who heard about this were greatly disturbed. From a homeless, itinerant preacher who had supposedly sacrificed all *for Jesus' sake*, Carroll now lived like a king; this development seemed anathema to every ideal of The Fellowship. If he had removed himself from the ministry this would probably not have been controversial, but he held onto the overseership while living at odds with fundamental tenets of the ministry, in direct contradiction of its basic doctrines. It was one rule for him, another for every other worker. Under the overseership of Carroll, the movement in Victoria became increasingly isolated from the rest of Australia. Rumblings within Victoria increased against Carroll, who responded with a wholesale scourge.

Week after week, friends were excommunicated. Whole meetings were put out, with many of the affected not even being informed of the reason. Children and teenagers were cast out along with their parents, even if they themselves were professing members. Many then exited themselves voluntarily in a show of solidarity with those ejected; this included my father and his eight siblings who left with my grandparents. The purge even extended into the state of South Australia, where many more were put out.

The Fellowship fractured, and at least three factions now existed - those loyal to Carroll (the official overseer of the state), those loyal to John Hardie (a senior worker of New South Wales at odds with Carroll's privileged lifestyle as overseer in Victoria), and those loyal to Edward Cooney (one of the founding workers previously excommunicated). Most of the disenfranchised continued their own fellowship meetings within their own faction; my father's family and their meeting continued to meet as part of the Hardie faction. This continued for some years until workers from overseas arrived to assist in straightening out the tangle. During this period of separation, they had their own annual Special Meeting and a separate convention at Mildura in the home of a Mrs Matz. Her very large home with enclosed verandas was set on a small rural property. Convention meetings were held by overseas workers during the day and families returned to their own homes each night; a situation that continued annually for possibly several years.

After the death of Carroll in 1953, many outcast friends were finally re-admitted to fellowship. A workers' meeting held at that time (Guildford NSW meeting, February 1954) agreed that Carroll had indeed acted contrarily to the beliefs and ideals of The Fellowship. But this conclusion, rather than re-unifying the factions, outraged those who had been faithful to Carroll, who felt that his life and witness had been tarnished. The conclusion was later 'unconditionally withdrawn' (April 1955). Although most meetings were reinstated to official standing, conventions were cancelled for a time to prevent the re-united factions coming into close contact, likely as a measure to prevent the already flammable situation from irretrievably combusting. New converts also needed to be shielded from this quagmire undergirding the *one true way*. Many dissensions and difficulties over the administration of Victoria and its relationship with the rest of Australia and even other nations continued to linger for years to come, a lasting legacy of Carroll's monarchic rule in Victoria.

However, the immediate troubles in Mildura were not over. Responding to the pleas of those who were cast out under Carroll's headship, Edward Cooney came to Mildura. One of the founding workers alongside William Irvine, Cooney was now an embarrassment and a problem, already excommunicated by British head workers, who had sent letters around the world stating that Cooney was now *persona non grata*, not to be welcomed into the homes of any of The Friends.

The founder William Irvine was also excommunicated in 1914, and his name was completely erased from the vocabulary of The Friends, under threat of excommunication. The legend of The Way being descended directly from apostolic origin with no human founder had been birthed, and was now being heralded across all continents outside of the British

Isles. Most of The Friends in Australia had not heard the name William Irvine, and the workers did everything in their power to keep it that way. Cooney, however, had known Irvine personally, and believed him to be a man God had used - through special revelation - to reinstate his Way on the earth. Already an outcast from the mainstream of The Fellowship anyway, Cooney had no vested interest in keeping the name of William Irvine a secret. He also claimed to have been converted and baptised at the age of seventeen, long before he met Irvine.[7] This was a direct denouncement of the 'Living Witness Doctrine', the Two-by-Two belief - made mandatory by Irvine around 1907 - that a person may only be saved by having direct contact with a worker of The Way. [8]

When Cooney was excommunicated, a contingent remained loyal to him. When he came to Mildura in the distressing days of the Carroll scourge, a faction clung to him. After Carroll's death, Cooney attempted to have this faction reinstated to official standing, but he was turned away from the workers' reconciliation meeting, along with his adherents. A separate Cooneyite group continues to this day in Mildura. Members of this tiny remnant are more the true bearers of the name 'Cooneyite' (they themselves shun this label) even though the Two-by-Twos in Australia are also often recognised by this name.

There is no doubt that all of these events, including the presence of Cooney, served to blacken the name of Mildura among faithful friends in other parts of the country. Could anything good ever come out of Mildura? It was indicated that there was deep, dark trouble at the heart of that place, and fear kept those who did not know the past from investigating any further. Fear also kept those who did know the past from speaking of it.

My father had grown up in this environment of intrigue, where the truth about matters was rarely spoken. After the troubles his family had been through, the lesson was well learnt - silence is golden. Nobody wanted to risk being alienated from The Way again, and therefore few dared ever speak of the matters which had caused the difficulties, even if ill feeling continued to smoulder. The names of Cooney and Irvine were not to fall from the lips of anyone in The Way again. Nor did they - publicly - until the publication of Doug & Helen Parker's expose book *The Secret Sect* thirty years later. So effective had the nullifying of the past been that the revelations of this book would shake many followers of The Way to the core; these reverberations would be felt across the world. Doug and Helen would be vilified and demonised. Many more members - obeying orders to burn copies of the book and not read it - remain ignorant even to this day.

I saw my Grandmother for the last time a few months before she died. She had always lived some distance from me, so I had not had many opportunities to see her in my childhood. As she approached the end of her life she moved even further away, to live with one of her daughters. I knew she would be bitterly disappointed that I had left The Way. At one point when it was believed she had only a short time to live, the extended family all travelled to see her. I had not seen her for years, and was keenly conscious of her disapproval and disappointment in me. I wanted to impress upon her that I had not forsaken God, but rather found Him. It proved to be an exceptionally difficult task. We were rarely alone in the house full of relatives. We took her out to lunch at a seafood café set in an old renovated warehouse, where the metal chairs and tables on wooden floorboards caused sound to reverberate loudly off every surface. With Grandma nearly deaf anyway, conversation seemed almost impossible. When I had the opportunity, I had to lean forward and almost shout in her ear to be heard.

'You know I left The Meetings...' I began. She immediately turned towards me.

'That was a terrible thing you did.' She responded sharply.

'But I want you to know – I have Jesus in my heart.'

She did not respond, and it was the last time we ever had opportunity to speak. A few months later we sat at her funeral and heard of her faithfulness to The Way.

Within weeks of her burial, my father wrote to the overseer in his state, and requested that the meeting be removed from his home. The overseer responded, asking if this could be delayed another three or four months over the convention season, until the start of the new year, when he would come to visit Dad personally and make arrangements. Dad agreed.

The overseer landed in Canberra, and arrived on Dad and Mum's doorstep, in the second last week of January, 2003. The fact that there was a doorstep to stand on was somewhat of a miracle. A few days before, on the 18th of January, an unprecedented firestorm had swept into Canberra from the mountains to the west. Over five hundred homes were wiped out, mostly in Dad and Mum's suburb and a few adjoining suburbs. My parents' home was the only structure still standing of all their neighbours. Scorched and somewhat forlorn, it stood as a lone survivor, windows blown inwards and bricks crumbling on the exterior from the intense heat.

The overseer arrived to be greeted by the still smouldering ruins of nearby homes and gardens in a monochromatic landscape of charcoal grey, where even the sky refused to oblige any colour. The air had been completely still for days, yielding a heavy grey mass of suspended smoke and ash which refused to dissipate. Dad and Mum had been away when the firestorm hit; they had not long returned home themselves. As they now all surveyed the lounge room - the former meeting room - there was little to say. The house was not fit for occupation. The meeting would have to be moved immediately; you could say it was fait accompli. Arrangements were quickly finalised, and Dad never went back to another meeting.

My parents were now nomads of sorts. They moved around for 3 years - housesitting, living with us and renting while repairs and rebuilding were carried out. They decided to incorporate a re-design and extension into the rebuilding of their home, and so when they finally moved back in, the old meeting room no longer existed. Even the exterior was no longer recognisable from the original. They came home to a new house and a new life, the memories of days past purged by fire.

---

7 In 1904 Edward Cooney preached about his conversion in 1884 at the age of 17. Cooney later accepted the 'Living Witness' Doctrine, only to reject it again in 1914. By 1916 he was accused of being 'out of step' with his brethren; one of the accusations levelled at him was the controversy of his insistence of conversion at age 17, which 'was many years before he began walking in the Truth [Two-by-Twos]'. *Edward Out of Step with his 'Brethren'* (Chapter 17, *The Life and Ministry of Edward Cooney* by Patricia Roberts).

8 *The 'Living Witness' Doctrine* (Chapter 9, *The Life and Ministry of Edward Cooney* by Patricia Roberts).

Making the News
23 September 2013

Protecting children – who cannot speak for themselves – should not and cannot be discretionary and it is not only our moral duty, it is now the law. We all must be alert to those circumstances that, unless properly managed, pose a threat to the welfare of our children.

- www.wingsfortruth.info

In September 2013 I was interviewed by Chris Johnston, senior writer and researcher for *The Age*, Melbourne, Australia. He was investigating the religious group behind child sexual assault charges pending in a Victorian court, the same group against whom a submission had been made to the Royal Commission for child sexual assault in Australia. Chris found it difficult to locate anyone from the group willing to be publicly identified or speak on the record, and I agreed to his request for an interview. The resulting article (*'Friends and Enemies, Truth and Lies'* by Chris Johnston, *The Age*, 23 September 2013) gave a very telling insight into the mentality still held by the overseer of Victoria, that despite no training in the field, and mandatory reporting requirements, he still feels fully qualified to investigate accusations himself, and pronounce them true or untrue.

Have I been sexually abused by the Two-by-Twos? No, I have not. Are the Two-by-Twos characterised by child sexual abuse? No, they are not. Overall, the number of perpetrators is hopefully few, and the overwhelming majority of The Friends would condemn such actions. Do the workers encourage sexual abuse in any way? I do not think so.

Do I know of many people who have been sexually abused by the Two-by-Twos? Yes, I do. Have any of them been officially reported? Some have, and the perpetrators have been convicted. But the number of known victims is far outnumbered by the victims who have not spoken out. When I count the number of cases that I know about through friends and acquaintances - officially unreported - I start to realise that the problem has been a quiet epidemic, a silent undercurrent along which many perpetrators have glided with impunity. If you believe I am exaggerating, please pay a visit to the *Wings for Truth* website, which is dedicated to assisting those who have been sexually abused within the Two-by-Twos. Through the personal stories of abuse survivors, a convincing picture emerges of a culture long practised in protecting The Way at all costs, silencing the abused and hiding the abusers. The Way has unwittingly become a perfect vehicle for child molestation.

Take a ministry with forced celibacy, and put it into homes where they have close and constant access to children and teenagers who are taught to obey and revere the workers. Add to this the propensity of some who *offer for the work* doing so to atone for past sins, and somehow seek to do penance, sometimes if not often for sexual sins. Add to this workers whose past sins are known to include molestation. Throw all of this into unsuspecting and unknowing families. Is this extreme naivety, or criminal culpability? Either way, it is already far too late for far too many individuals and their families.

And then there are the Two-by-Two parents who have committed these atrocious crimes against their helpless young. Affected children and teenagers who turned to workers for assistance were often turned away, sternly told to keep quiet about family secrets. If God's True Servants, those who must be obeyed and respected said that, then the victims must accept their lot, or believe that this behaviour was normal, or even right.

The evolved mentality of workers has developed into a self-ordained spiritual authority which places them somehow over and above the law in their own minds. It gives them the right to decide, on behalf of their members, not to involve the law, and has even allegedly gone so far, on occasion, as to forbid The Friends to report abuse, or give evidence in court against it. At the end of the day, the reputation of The Way is more important than anything else. The protection of the ministry is more important than the protection of children.

Agreeing to speak to *The Age* gave me no joy in having the Two-by-Twos represented as child molesters. I did not know anything about the worker mentioned in the article accused of molestation, and nothing of his guilt or innocence. I spoke publicly because of the cases I have heard about, for which there has not been justice. I spoke publicly because I want parents to think twice before leaving their children vulnerable to someone they have invited into their home, as the workers seem to have abrogated any responsibility on their part in this regard. I spoke publicly because the workers have knowingly put perpetrators into homes.

On 20 March 2014, the worker named in *The Age* pleaded guilty to nine counts of unlawful indecent assaults, gross assaults and gross indecency on three young female victims, some under twelve years of age at the time of the events. In June 2014 he was sentenced to some months in jail, most of them suspended, and expected to be incarcerated for 3 months.

Has justice been served? You would have to ask his victims. I admire the courage of those who have been brave enough to testify against any abuser in a court of law, and am thankful when they are vindicated by a guilty verdict. I am also saddened to be reminded that the effects of abuse will be profound and long lasting on those who have been abused, and know that justice only heals some wounds.

I do not name this worker because he is only one of many who have committed such abuses, and I see no reason to draw particular attention to the failings of this one man who has already been reported in the media. I continue to struggle with many aspects of this particular case. As pointed out, yes, these particular offences occurred before he went into the ministry of The Way. I believe that he himself informed the workers of his past when he went into the work, and there are indications that he sincerely sought to reform himself.

Several major problems are still evident here. The workers themselves should have reported this man to the authorities, or implored him to turn himself in. At the very least, they should have had pastoral concern for those who had been his victims. Instead, they appear to have kept it all very quiet and brought a known sex offender into the ministry. While this worker is the main offender, he had admitted some past offences to the worker ministry, and was looking to them as his spiritual and moral authority.

The next problem is that they knowingly sent him to stay in the homes of The Friends. I believe they did the offender a great dis-service here, not to mention The Friends themselves. Did his superiors insist that he not stay in homes with children? Did they inform elders in the area that he was never to stay in homes with children? Did they put any form of accountability in place? Or did they happily do the equivalent of putting the drunk in the bar every night, and assume everything would be fine? I believe the offender offered for the work of the ministry in good faith, probably wanting to put his past behind him or even do penance for it. The workers who accepted him seemed to care nothing about his past offences, justice for his victims, or temptations put to the offender in the future. They certainly cared even less about future potential victims. So yes, while this man remains the main offender here, the senior workers still have a lot to answer for. I can only hope that some valuable lessons have been learned from this whole sad saga.

The Cult Mentality

Any other preacher in the world can only be a preacher of death.

- Evan Jones, Australian Overseer (www.thelyingtruth.info)

The aftermath of the Two-by-Twos has been, for me, a long and protracted monster-under-the-bed mentality. You know in your head this monster is purely psychological, but that does not prevent fear still getting the better of you in an irrational way from time to time.

In the years since I have left, I have led a busy, happy and fulfilled life. But whenever I found myself recounting my past to anyone, tentacles of anxiety would unfurl from deep within, tightening my chest and quickening my pulse, and uncontrollable tremors would take hold of my body. I could not seem to prevent this physical process unravelling once again from its dark corner. It was not a spiritual response, but somehow an involuntary physical response to mental anguish re-visited yet again. For twenty years after leaving this continued to happen. It intensified during the writing of this book. After hours of recounting the past, the anxiety levels would reach fever pitch, and I would be a quivering mess. Multiple symptoms would return, and I would have to stop writing. In 2009 I developed Grave's Disease, an autoimmune illness usually triggered by extreme stress or trauma in individuals with a genetic predisposition. Although I am presently stable due to daily medication, stress is particularly apt to cause the disease to start spiralling out of control, so I tried to pace myself. After several cycles of writing, stress, anxiety, taking a break for a few days and then starting again, I reached a new resolve. I was heartily sick of this monster under the bed, snarling and waiting to grab me if I got too close. I finally acknowledged this potent being dwelling deep within my psyche just out of reach, which now and then reached up to claw at me yet again. I decided to confront this beast in a final showdown in the cold hard light of day. I dragged it out from under the bed and began to dissect it.

I started with the obvious questions. Why was it there? Why did I still experience these physical manifestations after so many years? Why wouldn't they go away? Was I still afraid of what I had done in leaving? Intellectually and spiritually, I knew I had no doubts about leaving, and the certainty has only ever become more certain as time has gone on. The greater the distance, the greater the perspective, and I have gained a clearer and clearer perspective of the Two-by-Twos, the further the distance between us. And yet despite my intellectual and spiritual freedom, my physical body continued to betray me, hinting at a still unrecognised mental bondage of some form. I suspected this wasn't just about the Two-by-Twos, but about the human condition; how it remembers and responds to former experience. I thought about survivors of terrible atrocities, and the mental and physical symptoms they suffer in the aftermath. I thought of a friend of mine who lived through terrorist acts, and still involuntarily dives under the table at the sound of a car misfiring. The mind and body seem to have a powerful ability to remember cause and effect at a deep cellular level that seems almost impossible to dislodge. Symptoms are triggered by memories.

Memories are triggered by the recurrence – in some form – of the original event, real or imagined.

What was my 'original event'? The most significant was the fear and physical manifestations that occurred when I first left the group. Whenever I revisited this event mentally, my body responded by going through the associated physical symptoms I suffered at the time. Realising this was comforting, but how to trip the circuit and cut off the power supply?

I decided to start a serious investigation on cults as never before. I had always balked at calling the Two-by-Twos a 'cult', as the word seemed so extreme. Now, I researched the nitty-gritty of mind control techniques and thought-stopping clichés. I read in-depth stories about experiences of others in groups where all seemed sweetness and light and genuine fellowship, and yet there was a malignancy that spread like cancer and showed up in the fruit of abuse, ostracism, judgmentalism, hypocrisy and ultimately a false gospel. I realised that the workers do not own the corner on this. Ex-members from any group with cult characteristics suffer as many of us from the Two-by-Twos have done. The fear and physical reactions I had were nothing unique. I had been mentally conditioned from a young age, and had believed and bought into everything I was told. I had broken free, but had not understood how I had been conditioned, and how it still affected me. Now, as I recognised the thought-stopping phrases I had been subjected to from my youngest years, I saw the flesh and bones and sinews of what makes up this monster, and the final vestiges of mystique were ripped away.

In the past year I recounted a large part of my story to someone, and discovered they had a very similar background – in another group. We laughed at the similarities in our language and understood each other's clichéd phrases about our lives and extended families. It was not until afterwards I realised the monster had not made an appearance. No uncontrollable tremors. No tightening of the chest. Suddenly the beast was gone. Probably because I ripped him apart, limb by limb, and carefully destroyed every piece. I no longer need to take a break from writing.

There is a social science fiction film called *The Truman Show* (1998), in which the protagonist, Truman, lives unknowingly in an artificial world created specifically for him. He is unknowingly the main character in a reality TV show, his every move watched by millions of viewers every day. Every other person around him is cast in a role, including his wife and best mate. Everything goes well for Truman as long as he behaves as he is expected to behave. Various manipulations are applied to prevent him from ever travelling beyond the set borders of his prescribed world. Everything is wonderful and safe and happy for Truman as long as he is unaware of the truth. Then he begins to notice strange things. He sees and discovers things he should not. His queries and attempts to discover what is going on are met with more and more desperate attempts to keep him under the ownership of his handlers.

When Truman started challenging the status quo, everything was at stake for those who had invested a lifetime in creating this artificial world. Truman eventually had to come to terms with discovering that his whole life was based on a lie. It seems more than a little familiar to me.

Being in the Two-by-Twos was very much like being Truman. Life could be good in our artificial world, our alternate reality. Everything was all right if we stuck to the script. However, I began to glimpse things behind the scenes. I disturbed the props. I asked difficult questions and interrupted the smooth running of the show.

Now an outsider of the Two-by-Twos, I relate more to the character of Sylvia. She was let into Truman's world as a cast member, but couldn't stand the deceit, and tried to tell Truman the truth. She was prevented and intercepted, and eventually forcibly removed from the set. Many of us ex Two-by-Twos are now Sylvia - desperate for the remaining Trumans to see behind the scenes for themselves and escape. But there remains a vast cast who are intent on perpetuating their artificial world for their own financial support, contentment and happiness, and who genuinely believe in its purpose.

It is often thought that people who belong to a sect or cult are mentally deficient - simpletons or zombies who cannot think for themselves. I would beg to differ. Cult members are not zombies. They are often intelligent and articulate - normal people with normal lives - well able to function at all levels of professional vocation. This said, it must also be admitted that many cults, including the Two-by-Twos, view education with suspicion and tend to have a stronger hold in rural communities where members are less practised in the disciplines of intellectual rigour.

No matter how smart or thoughtful the cult member may be, they remain in the group because their thinking processes are constantly quashed. Cult members would be insulted to be told they do not think for themselves. Yes, they do think for themselves, but only to the boundaries permitted. After that, their thought-stopping techniques kick in to prevent them from losing their 'faith'; that is, faith in their group.

The Way is perfect, but the people aren't ...
If I doubt I'll give the devil a foothold ...
All honest, seeking, sincere souls are led to this Way ...
We have the only true ministry ...

They have had years of training, reinforced repeatedly, to stop any thought outside the leader mandated safety zone. They mentally and unwittingly recite core messages such as the ones shown above as an insurance policy against doubt. For the most part, they will continue to make decisions based on what will be approved by the leaders rather than any personal convictions. If they do act against the approval of the leaders, they will generally keep their actions secret and live a kind of double life, not willing to 'stir up trouble' by living more openly as they would wish.

People who get caught up in cults do so for many and varied reasons, often tied to a general disillusionment with life rather than an inability to think. They stumble upon a certain group, seeking meaning and security, and are told it was meant to be. Two-by-Twos believe that the *honest, seeking soul* will find The Way if they are seeking *God's true way* hard enough. Newcomers become settled and comfortable well before they realise they are slowly being conditioned to mental captivity.

Many cult members, of course, are born in this captivity and conditioned for life. No compound is needed, as mental incarceration often has a far greater hold than physical incarceration.

All cult members quickly learn that there are many advantages to living in captivity. Leaders make and enforce the rules and keep members safe in the confines of the group. They feel relieved not to have to live in the jungle *out there in the world*, fending for themselves, trying to discern right and wrong. Leaders act as spiritual 'parents', making the rules and decisions for their spiritual 'children' and punishing them for their disobedience.

The sense of community and camaraderie in such groups is often very strong, and family ties become enmeshed through multiple connections. Cults have a sense of purpose and belonging often lacking in modern society. It is akin to belonging to a huge tribe, with its own customs and traditions. The wellbeing of the tribe is jealously guarded, and outsiders are viewed with suspicion and kept at arm's length. 'Loyalty unto death' and 'us against the world' mentalities exist in groups that take their membership the most seriously, with cults and gangs at the forefront. Both also share a common bond in their dismissiveness of law. Gangs operate outside it, while cults believe they are above it. In an environment where cult leaders claim to have the very authority of God, they make the rules, rules that 'the world' does not understand. When called on to explain themselves and their organisation to outsiders, cult leaders tend to have a very elastic interpretation when explaining who they are, what they do and how much money is involved. This seems especially to be the case when such leaders are called upon to answer to government requirements, legal responsibility and ethical accountability.

The Two-by-Twos as a whole continue to claim they are not an organisation, and not a religion. If any of the workers are called upon by authorities as ministers of the group, they quickly respond that they are 'not ordained ministers', seeking to absolve themselves of any form of accountability, including mandatory reporting requirements. Yet they have registered themselves as an organisation in a number of countries, under a number of names, a fact that they strenuously continue to deny to lay members. [9]

For the recovering cult member, it takes a long time to unravel and straighten out the twists and tangles created by many years of conditioning woven unceasingly into their life. Typical trademarks of the cult member are loyalty and faithfulness, and these traits are often exhibited towards the leaders every bit as much as - or even more than - to God. For people who believe they love God and want to honour him, separating this love of God from entanglement with a controlling group is extremely difficult. Those who are able to leave physically are often still chained mentally and continue to be held in spiritual bondage. Many will never seek another church, having been conditioned against them for so long. Some may eventually return to the cult after some years on the outside, often out of guilt. They will be warmly welcomed back into the fold, their return providing a great morale boost for long-term members. Returnees will experience a short-term spiritual high before the reality of striving to be worthy sets back in, and they realise yet again that they will never measure up.

Cults seem to develop their own series of stories designed to demonstrate to followers that their Way is, without any doubt, the *one true way*. These stories become urban legend, recounted to each other repeatedly with awe, to remind themselves of their special honour in belonging to the group, and pitying those who are outside, or who have fallen away from the faith.

A favourite story in the Two-by-Twos consists of someone living all alone in a remote place, waiting and praying for God's true messengers to come to them. Sometimes they wait for years, but the workers finally come and knock on their door, and they just know straight away that these are the true messengers that they have been praying for, and this is the one true way.

Another well-known story consists of a worker coming into the presence of *a false spirit* - either in a medium/fortune teller, or perhaps a clergyman of a mainstream Christian denomination - where the person with the 'false spirit' is suddenly rendered speechless and powerless in the presence of a worker, who obviously wields enormous spiritual power and authority.

Perhaps the most commonly told story is that of those who left The Way, only to die a week or two later, usually in a car accident. There are many variations of this tale, and according to Two-by-Two folklore, an inordinately high number of people have apparently died in strange accidents very soon after daring to leave The Way. This story is particularly effective in retaining members and instilling fear. I hasten to add that this story is superstitious; the workers do not threaten or carry out physical harm against their members or those who leave.

In 1994 the Two-by-Twos in Australia came under police and media scrutiny in the most tragic and confronting of circumstances. At Pheasant Creek near Kinglake, in the state of Victoria, two children - Narelle

Henderson (14 years old) and her brother Stephen (12 years old) - committed suicide by shooting themselves with a rifle just before they were due to attend their annual convention. Narelle left a suicide note stating 'We committed suicide because all our life we were made to go to meetings. They tried to brainwash us so much and have ruined our lives.'[10] While it is very difficult to know all the circumstances surrounding this particular tragedy, it cast an immediate spotlight on the group and its practices, and sent shudders through the Two-by-Twos worldwide.

It is worth noting that the majority of cults do not knowingly organise themselves as a cult or purposely set out to learn mind control techniques. Yet a similar set of behavioural characteristics are fostered in these types of groups the world over, founded by a zealous belief set and authoritarian leadership. What is the main difference between genuine Christianity and the Bible-based cult? I believe that in genuine Christianity, people are more important than the system. In cults, the system takes priority over people.

A cult does not seek to protect people or minister to the wounded soul, it always firstly seeks to protect its own mindset and belief system. It originates with a zealous conviction of what is needed – generally a 'new order' of some type, or a 'return to original principles' – and ends with a strident system that protects itself at all costs, to the personal cost of followers.

Conversely, Jesus did not seem concerned about protecting the rules or reputation of any man-made system. He cared first about individuals, and their physical and spiritual needs, at the cost of any established religious order. As we read through the gospels, we notice that Jesus often provoked controversy by acting outside the accepted religious norms. He 'broke' certain Sabbath traditions because they were man-made, putting people into further bondage. Leaders nit-picked his healing of the sick because in doing so he stepped outside the carefully established system.

We see clearly that the 'system' as a whole did not respond well to Jesus. His own people did not officially recognise him as Messiah; rather, they rejected him, and put him to death. To the established Jewish religious authorities of that time, their system of rules and hierarchy of authority was of first priority and they would protect it at any cost.

Those who did respond to Jesus in faith did not do so through the 'official' religious channels of the day, but as individuals. Jesus called whomever he chose, however he chose, and they believed and followed him. They testified of him, and witnessed about him. It is an important lesson for us. No religious structure, no particular church, no *Way*, has the authority to declare whom Jesus has saved. And wherever a system is protected while the needs of the people to whom it ministers are trampled on, it has lost sight of its ultimate purpose and is treading on dangerous ground.

Cults often see the world in black and white, where all people are either *in* or *out* of their particular organisation; by default this makes them in or out of favour with God. This is at odds with genuine Christian churches who do not seek to judge any individual's faith on the basis of whether or not they attend a particular church. They may challenge a person's personal commitment to faith based on their actions, but if a person has simply stopped attending a particular church, they are not judged to be *out* of *the right way*.

Churches, of course, have an exceptionally important role to play in the life of Christians. They facilitate worship, provide genuine teaching and exposition of the Bible, and provide spiritual oversight and leadership of the local congregation. Leaders within the church do these things as those accountable to God, and in the understanding that ultimately Christians are responsible in working out their own salvation; that is, members of the congregation are Christians because they accept God's free gift of salvation by grace in Jesus Christ, not because they belong to a particular group or church. Each Christian has the working of the Holy Spirit within them, and in the end are personally accountable to God, not to man. A good church will challenge its members to live a life of genuine faith with personal integrity before God, with a central focus on the foundational truth of the gospel - that Jesus alone is the justifier and sanctifier of all believers, regardless of which church they belong to, or how they came to faith. Justification through the life and death of Christ as Saviour leaves no room for any type of system which sets itself up in any form to add some other variant of 'necessity' to the gospel. Any such system has to be denounced - at best as spiritual pride, and at worst as heresy.

We see such a variant in cults, where personal faith becomes subject to an earthly spiritual authority, through which personal faith must now be channelled. Spiritual authoritarians in cult leadership practise an over-zealous 'watchman' mentality; people cannot be trusted to be personally accountable to God in their walk of faith. They must therefore be monitored, controlled, punished for deviation. Cult leaders must be assured not of their members' full commitment to God, but to the cult. Because members are forced to acknowledge that true faith cannot exist outside the group, they know their own faith is heavily reliant upon subjection to its leaders.

This spiritual subjection may cause cult members to experience a serious disconnect between their 'spiritual' life and 'real' life as two planes of existence. In their spiritual life, they attend regular gatherings where they seek to conform to cult expectations, and then return to their real life, which consists of everyday living and working, and interactions with outsiders away from the immediate influence and authority of leaders. These two planes of existence may have little to do with each other, creating a cognitive dissonance. Some cults seek to overcome this difficulty with permanent communal living. Perhaps many in the Two-by-Twos gain some relief from this dissonance during their annual convention.

[9] For further information on registered names of the Two-by-Twos, see www.tellingthetruth.info/lists/church_names.php

[10] As stated in *Friends and Enemies, Truth and Lies* by Chris Johnston, The Age, Fairfax Media, 23 September 2013. Original source unknown.

The 'Gospel' of the Workers

I am astonished that you are so quickly deserting the one who called you to live in the grace of Christ and are turning to a different gospel - which is really no gospel at all.

- Galatians 1:6-7 9 (NIV)

A question I am often asked these days in relation to my past association with the Two-by-Twos is 'did you use the Bible?' Shamefaced, I admit that we did, and wait for the inevitable follow-up query. 'How then didn't you know the gospel?'

Good question. The Two-by-Twos do not see Jesus as who he really is. They are still operating under an Old Testament mindset, relying heavily on a man-oriented ministry, trying to keep their own laws and trying to be found good enough in their own efforts. What, really, has changed for them in the fact that Christ has come? Why do they need him at all? If salvation is obtainable by obeying the Law, they have no use for a saviour. Indeed, most reject him as their saviour, claiming instead that he is the 'perfect example', the benchmark by which we must live and be judged.

The Two-by-Twos, like many cults, have set themselves up as the only true spiritual authority, not the Bible. Everything in the Bible is filtered by the group leaders, who give their own interpretation and definition of everything therein. Mind, conscience and logical powers of thinking are often surrendered to groups such as The Fellowship. Of course, this can bring much disquiet if serious issues arise, but few are willing to stick their head above the parapet and attract attention for having *a wrong spirit*, which denotes that you are not acting in the best interests of the group; by implication you are being selfish by damaging its reputation. The reputation of the system is everything - *The Way is perfect.* If you have a problem, it is you who are deficient in some way.

After leaving The Fellowship and attending a new church for some time, it dawned on me that ministers of Christian churches rarely if ever mention themselves. If they do, it is usually to confess their own shortcomings and need of grace.

The workers, on the other hand, talk of almost nothing but themselves. Where ministers use the Bible to point to Christ and to expound the gospel, workers look for ways to have it point to themselves - their work of ministry, their religious format. While ministers constantly point to the sacrifice of Jesus, workers constantly point to their own sacrifice of *forsaking all.* Despite workers claiming that they are the most humble and lowly of all God's servants on earth, they sure do spend a lot of time talking about themselves and directing attention away from Christ. In constantly pointing people to their own ministry and efforts, the workers neglect the actual message of the gospel. The envelope has become far more important than the message it is supposed to carry. Somewhere along the way, the message has fallen out, and the envelope is now empty.

The workers have inadvertently created another Old Testament Levitical priesthood, standing between the people and God, 'sacrificing' themselves to bring people to God, and trying, by their own efforts and the efforts of The Friends, year after year, to make themselves good enough to stand before God. They have created the same type of ministry that Jesus came to completely do away with. By continually pointing to their ministry, they are continually pointing to themselves, and away from Jesus. To all who look at the workers and say 'here is The Way', Jesus says no, 'I am the way, the truth and the life. No one comes to the Father except through me.' (John 14:6)

The main difference for me now is that my faith is my own - at its core it is independent of any earthly authority. Previously, my faith was inextricably linked to the group to which I belonged - my faith was in the group itself, and could not exist except in co-existence with the group.

Since I left, I have belonged to a local protestant church congregation. David and I decided to continue attendance at the same church in which he grew up, the same church that was integral to my own coming to faith. We now have many years of history within this congregation, and they are our spiritual family. It is geographically close - within our own neighbourhood - and we are able to host a Sunday morning Bible study prior to the Sunday morning worship service. While travelling or on holidays we attend services at various denominations, dependent on what churches exist in the area. We enjoy friendship and fellowship with a wide acquaintance of Christians who belong to many different congregations and denominations, and rejoice to know that God is at work in many ways and places and types of administration, but the same Spirit is at work in all.

So much of life has had to be relearned. My expression of faith has had to undergo significant rehabilitation. One example is praise and worship, which was an entirely new concept to me. In church services, we come together as a community of God's people to worship him together. Many psalms, hymns and songs are sung as an expression of this worship. In past Two-by-Two meetings, I do not recall much about praise or worship. We met together in small home groups to give testimonies, expressing our shortcomings and how to be more worthy, and give thanks for being in The Way. In mission meetings we listened to the workers talk continually about themselves as the only true ministry, the perfection of The Way, and that we must keep walking in it. We sang about Jesus, but rarely in worship to him. In my experience, the terms 'hallelujah' or 'praise the Lord' were anathema to The Friends.

In my new life, to be Christian is to confess Christ as Lord, and to seek personal holiness in every area of life, having a personal relationship with God and responding to him out of faith and personal conviction. Many Christians work in various areas of Christian ministry. Others use their money for the Kingdom of God. Not just in supporting the ministry of the local church, but also in Word and deed ministries - financially and prayerfully supporting other ministries and organisations as they seek to bring the Gospel of Christ to the world and as they also seek to relieve suffering and provide assistance to the poor and needy. Word (The Word of God) and deed (assistance) together are imperative - we cannot preach the Gospel to hungry and needy people without caring about their physical and mental welfare. Neither should we care only for their physical needs without also being concerned with their eternal wellbeing. Yes, these are our works as Christians. As the Bible so eloquently expresses, 'The work of God is this: to believe in the one he has sent.' (John 6:29); and 'If one of you says to them, 'Go in peace; keep warm and well fed,' but does nothing about their physical needs, what good is it?' (James 2:16).

To the best of my knowledge, The Fellowship is not involved in relieving the sufferings of their fellow man. Instead, they appear to actively discourage such actions. Firstly, they claim that 'the poor you will always have with you', interpreting these words of Jesus to mean that poor and needy people are an unfortunate fact of life, and we shouldn't be distracted by them. Some workers have even gone so far as to suggest that they themselves are the poor and needy to which Jesus referred, as they have forsaken everything for their form of ministry. Therefore, The Friends are fulfilling their mission to the poor and needy of the world by feeding, clothing and housing the workers. Most convenient for all concerned, I must say, a mutually beneficial arrangement.

Those who leave The Fellowship can find it extremely difficult to commit themselves to a mainstream Christian congregation, or even attend a church service inside a church building. Many step out from The Fellowship with no faith in God whatsoever. After apparently striving so hard for so long in their faith, how can this be?

Perhaps their faith was like temperamental unstable oil within the vessel of their soul. It took careful handling to keep the conditions just right for the oil to survive without becoming rancid, ineffective. Their faith was kept in a cold, dark place to keep it perfectly intact without contamination from the light and heat of the world. Perhaps their faith did become intolerably rancid, or perhaps they were just plain weary of trying to maintain its quality while being subject to so many inconsistencies. When they left, they recognised that their faith was useless – it only worked under strictly controlled conditions. They tipped out this useless oil and their vessel is now completely empty.

For others, they do have a personal relationship with God, and are growing in their understanding of true faith. The water of life has been slowly filling their vessel, even though the oil of religious compliance remains visible on the surface. As the water rises, there is less room for the oil, which starts to overflow and be lost. Oil and water – religious conformity and the true living water of faith in Christ alone. They may co-exist, but it is the religious conformity that will be most visible to others, and yet the least effective. For some, the oil thins so much that the water of true faith has started to overflow, and is now becoming visible to all. It will not be tolerated for long by cult authorities, and the owners of such vessels will need to find a new spiritual home.

Perhaps you are a former member of this particular group - or another cult - who has left and simply don't know where to go to church or who to trust. Perhaps you are a former member who has rejected God by virtue of rejecting the cultic authorities you were formerly under, and you want nothing more to do with either. Perhaps you still belong to a highly controlling group but are not satisfied in your faith.

I would implore you to seek Christ directly - not another 'way'. Your Bible is the best place to start, and there are some excellent group Bible studies available, which anyone can attend without being attached to a particular church denomination. One of the most widely recognised programs is Bible Study Fellowship (BSF - www.bsfinternational.org/locate-a-class1) - see if you can find one underway near you. Another study program is Know Your Bible (KYB – www.cwciaus.org.au). I would strongly encourage you to undertake further Bible study through a strong program no matter where you are at right now – whether you are attending The Meetings or not, attending another church or not.

The Two-by-Twos appear, on the surface, harmless and benign; a quaint people who hold to old-fashioned ways. Perhaps they arouse a desire for a simpler way of life, or nostalgia for days past when life was less complicated than our modern era. There are no bizarre rituals, condoned perverse activities or secret rites. Members are mostly genuine in seeking to live out their faith in a simple, humble way. It all seems so attractive, so right.

And yet, despite all claims to the contrary, at their heart is considerable worldliness. While leaders keep a tight rein on all aspects of meeting together and external appearances, there is a significant lack of understanding of sin, replaced by rule-keeping and conformity of behaviour. 'Such regulations indeed have an appearance of wisdom, with their self-imposed worship, their false humility and their harsh treatment of the body, but they lack any value in restraining sensual indulgence.' (Colossians 2:23 NIV.) There is compliance to a dress code and lifestyle, but little in the way of genuine care towards the poor and needy. There is no ability to discern true godliness or principles of holiness or a genuine Christian worldview. Members often fall prey to every prevalent scam due to this lack of discernment and lack of practice in working through issues for themselves. They are sitting ducks for every pyramid scheme or sales scheme that claims it is the only way to live, has the only products worth buying, has the only cosmetics that are completely safe.

Many members are completely zealous in their desire to serve God as well as they possibly can, *doing their best*, obeying the rules with a determined passion and a *willing spirit*. They genuinely seek to do what is right - according to the workers - in most areas of life.

Others appear zealous, but prove that even perfect external conformity to The Way can be coupled with shady business deals, tax evasion and chronic traffic violations. These issues of the heart and of sin are lightly dismissed as *cares of the world* and therefore unworthy of serious examination in the light of a personal spiritual life.

For the less zealous, members are often looking to what they can get away with without attracting attention from the workers or receiving the criticism of having *a wrong spirit*. Blatantly disregarding any attempt at holy living is just fine as long as no one finds out.

I have come across a number of long standing Two-by-Twos who claim not to believe in The Way at all; they just continue to 'go along with it'. They are held fast by the unbreakable bonds of family, loyalty, time, familiarity, belonging. They were born into this tribe, have no significant ties outside it, and cannot even begin to comprehend losing their entire culture if they were to leave. The cost is too great, the outside too unfamiliar.

For some who leave, it's out of the frying pan and into the fire. Because they are seeking 'another Way' rather than individual faith, they fall prey to other groups with cultic overtones. For others, deep trust issues linger, and they remain permanently unable to join any church, unwilling to put themselves under any kind of spiritual headship ever again.

More recently I have had the great blessing of coming into contact with members of the Two-by-Twos who do understand the true message and gospel of Christ, and recognise that I do too. They do not reject me by virtue of being 'out', and are not afraid to maintain contact and discuss theological issues.

Such people seem to have a clear and beautiful picture of Jesus within the framework of The Fellowship of the friends and workers. But they appear to be an aberration from the broader group. I say this in the best possible way, and am greatly encouraged that they want to discuss faith and scripture, and how to be encouraged and grow in it. For most of us who have left, it is a sad reality that the majority of The Friends are unprepared or unwilling to discuss spiritual issues. While in the Two-by-Twos, I had only a frame - no picture. A system of faith, but no true understanding of the sacrifice of Jesus. When I finally heard and understood the true gospel of grace, this new picture of Christ wouldn't fit the frame I already had. The picture became more important to me than the frame, and the workers said I couldn't have both, so I took the picture and had to leave the frame behind.

The ultimate irony is that the Two-by-Two ministry, which claims to be the only one not man-made, is exactly that. The Friends do not believe ultimately in Jesus as the way of salvation, they believe in their ministry - a system - as the way of salvation. Take away the method of ministry, and what gospel remains? For them, the frame will always be more important than the picture. The method will always be more important than the message.

Many will accuse me of laying blame on the Two-by-Twos in matters where other churches are guilty of the same things. Yes, other churches are full of sinful, faulty human beings and imperfect pastors. Church structures and authority figures have and will continue to fail church members in many ways. So why pick on the Two-by-Twos? Why go on and on about their every failing?

Where do I start? The continued denial and cover-up of sexual abuse within the Two-by-Two system is only part of a much larger picture of an organisation where their lack of true pastoral care is evidenced in their callous disregard of genuinely hurting souls. Forced divorces are commanded if any divorced member dares re-marry and wants to continue in the group or re-join the group after leaving. Members are excommunicated and cast out for disagreeing with a worker, while friends and workers who have committed serious crimes of sexual abuse are protected within the group. No financial visibility or accountability is ever provided to The Friends regarding money from members and deceased estates which is stashed in hidden bank accounts. But none of this, serious as it is, is the fundamental problem.

The most serious indictment against the Two-by-Twos is that they claim to be the only way to God, even though their very foundation is based on deceit. They claim that their *Way* is perfect. They claim exclusive spiritual authority, and relentlessly coerce their members to believe only in them and their system. They bind people to them through fear and conditioning. More than that - they preach a false gospel, claiming that they alone are The Way and The Truth, and that life has to be lived their way to be acceptable to God. They deny that Jesus alone can bear these titles.

I did not leave the Two-by-Two way to follow another way. I did not escape the doctrine of the workers to follow the doctrines of other men. I left The Way because I met Jesus. He showed me that faith cannot be dependent on any human being, ministry, church or organisation. He showed me that what I had been following previously was called 'the way' and 'the truth', but was in fact a lie. He alone is 'the way, the truth and the life' (John 14:6).

Abundant Life

I seek a place that can never be destroyed, one that is pure, and that fadeth not away, and it is laid up in heaven, and safe there, to be given, at the time appointed, to them that seek it with all their heart. Read it so, if you will, in my book.

- John Bunyan, The Pilgrim's Progress

I often tell people that God dragged me into his kingdom kicking and screaming. I thought I had it all worked out when I professed my faith in The Way at age 16, but my plans were interrupted by God. He forced my hand and brought me out - initially - most unwillingly. He did many miracles along the way, but that is nothing for a God who can do anything he chooses. The greatest miracle of God is the turning of stubborn and unwilling hearts to himself. Every life committed to Christ is a miracle, an amazing story of grace and unfathomable love.

I have been accused by some over the years of choosing 'the easy way out', that is, The Friends believe it is easier to leave The Way than to stay in it and continue the struggle of 'being faithful'. To those people I say 'try it, and then tell me that it's easier'. Leaving was the hardest thing I have ever done.

God's work in our lives is not over until our life's journey is ended. He continues to interrupt my life with the unexpected. David and I discovered, after three years of marriage, that we would not be able to have children. After marriage, we had happily settled into domesticity together, looking at our own blueprint and making plans for a family. It never occurred to us that God had a different blueprint, but he did. While it was difficult news to adjust to, there were also clear indications that through many circumstances God had prepared me for this all along. We continue to be amazed at the happiness he has blessed us with in bringing us together. I've had to learn to be content knowing that his plans bring us far greater blessing than our own plans. It's a lesson I'll have to continue to learn, because life continues to be full of unexpected twists and turns.

The most important lesson I have learnt is that life isn't about striving to be worthy enough for God. It is about being in a relationship with him, right now and every day. It is about living for him in ways that intersect in the lives of real people in real ways. Obedient service to God is not about wearing our hair a certain way or wearing the right shoes. It is about caring and providing for others, helping the widow and the orphan, ministering to those in prison. It is about loving and sharing with those who don't know Christ, instead of avoiding them because they look different from us.

Do I do all these things well, and consistently? No, of course not. I continue to be an imperfect, faulty human being. I continue to battle against pride and selfishness and a host of other sins. I am no better than anyone else; God forbid that I should ever think that I am.

Where am I now? After a number of years in public service doing finance and business administration, I left to work part-time, and then full-time – in a Christian school. Initially teaching art and textiles, I have since become a full time finance officer and administrator. Working with a Christian staff where we commence each morning with singing and prayer together is an amazing blessing to have in a workplace.

I have also been extremely privileged and blessed in my long-term work as a Crossroad Bible Institute instructor - marking lessons and writing letters to prison inmates across Australia, Fiji and Papua New Guinea who do Bible correspondence courses through this Institute. I often feel far more blessed by them and their input to these lessons than they could possibly be by my input. What encouragement these men and women are to my faith - I strongly commend this work to you, which also operates out of many other places in the world, including the master base in America.

What of the man I married? I continue to be immeasurably blessed and amazed that God brought David into my life. He has gone on to do many things - full time work with the Australian Navy (as a civilian), where he is also involved in the Military Christian Fellowship and current editor of the Christian Defence magazine 'Crossfire'. He is a talented landscape photographer and wedding photographer, creating special opportunities for us to travel. In the past year he completed his second master's degree while simultaneously serving as an elder in the church, running a Sunday morning Bible study and taking on additional part-time work as a charter bus driver (for fun) and marking assessment items for other university students doing their master's (also for fun). He leaves me breathless in his wake.

And yet most of all he is a true man of God. A man of faith and integrity, but also in continual service to others - he will never say no to a request for help, and will go two miles for any man who asks him to go one. This is the extraordinary man God gave me, who constantly continues to teach me what true godliness is by his life of service to others.

I commenced this book expressing anger at The Way at the time of my grandfather's funeral. And yet I'm not angry at the workers. We wrestle not against flesh and blood, but against the powers and principalities of darkness (Ephesians 6). I'm angry at their chains of bondage, with which both they and their followers are bound. At the foundation of their beliefs is fundamental deceit about their origins, which continues to permeate many aspects of their ministry.

More than this, the workers are more to be pitied than most men, having sacrificed their lives on the altar of a works-righteousness gospel, which is really no gospel at all. My heart aches for them, and I desperately pray they, too, will find the fullness of freedom in Christ.

The process of writing this book has been decidedly lengthy. I initially commenced writing it twenty years ago, not long after leaving the Two-by-Twos. Various events then instigated spasmodic periods of writing over the years. These writings finally evolved into a fully-fledged book only in the last eighteen months prior to publication (2013-2015).

The decision to put all that has happened into a book for the scrutiny of others is no small decision, and I still agonise over it to some extent. Autobiographical writing requires the unveiling of difficult self-truths, and the writer is apt to struggle with the temptation of a subjective and self-flattering perspective. Very personal content has to be included for posterity and validity, and yet much is also often withheld for the sake of privacy and personal relationships. How much to reveal and how much to withhold is a delicate balance, and I hope I have shared enough to make this worthwhile to the reader.

While I generally find self-exposure uncomfortable, I felt compelled to write this book that others may know they are not alone. Perhaps others have known the intensity of what I have shared in this book. Perhaps their spiritual foundations have been shattered and they are still trying to find their foothold. Perhaps some are still struggling with vestiges of mental bondage. Perhaps some of us who have left can't adequately express to others what it was that we went through.

I hope this book can be a comfort or help if you - or those you love - have undergone similar experiences. Ultimately, though, my greatest desire is that those who have been under a false gospel may understand - perhaps even for the first time - the true Gospel of the Lord Jesus Christ. It is the free gift of salvation for which the price has already been paid, if only we will repent and believe. This means repentance of all our sin, including the pride that causes us to think we can earn our way to heaven. 'For it is by grace you have been saved, through faith - and this is not from yourselves, it is the gift of God, - not by works, so that no one can boast' (Ephesians 2:8-9).

This is not cheap grace, as the workers may assert; it is very, very expensive grace. To believe that our own works or sacrifices can earn or contribute to this gift is the greatest offense to the one who has already paid the greatest price for it.

Acknowledgements

So many have been very generous with their praise, support and advice on my manuscript, not to mention their time on very valuable proofreading and editing – Bill Bosker, Ron & Lyn Coleman, Joan Daniel, Kevin Daniel, Helen Parker, Peter and Lindy Gadsby, Cherrie and Gordon Harriss, Margaret James, Cherie Kropp, the Whitsunday crew (Jenni and Sue!) and Jen Miller of Christian Editing Services.

So many others have had such an impact on my spiritual life or been involved with the events of this book, and I feel obliged to mention them here.

Doug and Helen Parker, for their significant effort in putting together *The Secret Sect*, a book that continues to open the eyes of many and reveal historical truth. Thank you for your friendship and support over many years. I was most thankful for the blessing of seeing Doug for the last time just a few weeks prior to his passing at Easter 2014.

Joan Daniel, Kevin Daniel, Daurelle Chapman, Lloyd Fort, Kathy Lewis, Lynn Cooper. Your revealing and informative books have helped so much in releasing many from bondage to fear, including myself.

Cherie Kropp, for her unceasing and tireless work on sourcing, researching and maintaining historical records on the Two-by-Twos, and writing a comprehensive account of the life and ministry of William Irvine. Her work of preservation of historical truth will be invaluable for coming generations. Thank you for your continued friendship and advice.

Forum friends on *The Liberty Connection* and *Truth Meetings Boards*; Facebook friends on '*ex members of the*

2x2's; Cooneyites; Way; Secret Sect; Truth; Friends etc,' '*The Secret World of Truth'*, '*Professing Open Air'*, '*Professing Bible Believers'*. All of you have enriched my life with your personal convictions, quest for truth and hearty debate. Above all, you are willing to enter into the conversation.

Many dear friends in Sydney and Mildura who also left during the exodus of the 90s, along with other members of the Gladesville Anglican church in Sydney with whom we formed deep bonds of friendship. Long weekends spent together at Katoomba Christian Convention over many years formed our 'de-briefing' years, and will never be forgotten.

Dave McDonald, evangelistic preacher extraordinaire for many years at university campuses in Canberra, cancer survivor, and author – thank you for opening my eyes to the truth of the gospel.

Reverend Bill Bosker for his part in bringing me to Christ, and who, along with his wife Inneke provided so much support and wisdom through my darkest days.

Chris Johnston, senior writer for The Age, Fairfax media, Melbourne Australia. For his research, interest and reporting on sexual abuse issues within the Two-by-Two ministry in Victoria, Australia. Your work of bringing this information to public awareness has given many more people the courage to speak out.

My parents-in-law, Ron & Lyn Coleman, for their acceptance, encouragement, wisdom and advice over four long years of an unorthodox courtship with their son. For instilling in their children the importance of faith, commitment and integrity.

My parents, Gordon and Cherrie Harriss, for their continued love throughout our spiritual separation. For their courage to grasp truth when it was revealed to them, and launch out from all they had ever known to start life again outside The Two-by-Twos.

My husband David, my best friend who never ceases to broaden my horizons with his love of adventure and generosity of soul. The man God gave me, for which I will be forever thankful.

Photos

Photos associated with this book are available at:
www.culttochristbook.com
www.facebook.com/pages/Elizabeth-Coleman-Cult-to-Christ-Book/1422568694725497

Further Reading

Books

A Search for the Truth by Lloyd Fortt
Reflections Compiled by Daurelle Chapman
Reflected Truth Compiled by Joan F Daniel
Reinventing the Truth by Kevin N Daniel
The Church With No Name by Lynn Cooper
The Church Without a Name by Kathleen Lewis
The Secret Sect by Doug and Helen Parker
"Two by Two", The shape of a Shapeless Movement by Irvine
        Grey
The Life and Ministry of William Irvine by Cherie Kropp
        (www.tellingthetruth.info/founder_book)

For a full list of books and other publications regarding the
Two-by-Twos, see www.tellingthetruth.info/lists/books.php

Websites

www.tellingthetruth.info
www.wingsfortruth.info
www.thelyingtruth.info
professing.proboards.com (Truth Meetings Board forums)
veteransoftruth.blogspot.com
www.votisalive.com
www.workersect.org

Facebook Groups

(Some of these may be Closed Groups; members need to
apply for access). The Secret World of Truth; Professing –
Open Air; 323 Youth; Professing Bible Believers

The White Envelopes

A Short Story

One day a strange thing happened. I had an envelope delivered to me by a postman who insisted that the letter enclosed was only valid if the envelope was white, the only correct colour for envelopes. I took the pile of envelopes from the postman, selected the white envelope and opened the enclosed letter. It read 'You know that this letter is correct because you got it from a white envelope.' The rest of the page was blank. I turned it over and checked the back, which was blank as well.

'Where's the message?' I asked. The postman looked dumbfounded.

'That IS the message!' he insisted. 'Look, it's in a white envelope!'

'This message doesn't tell me anything!' I cried. 'How do I find out more?'

The postman scratched his head. 'Um, well, I dunno. I guess you gotta subscribe'.

'How do I subscribe?'

'Well, I'm not really authorised to tell you. You'll need to come down to the post office and they can explain it.'

'What will I be subscribing to?'

'The guaranteed delivery of only white envelopes. That way you can keep getting the correct message.'

'What do I do with all these white envelopes?'

'Keep them! Protect them and care for them. Try to keep them pristine. Find a place of reverence for them in your home. Prop them up on display somewhere important, where you can always be reminded of their presence.'

'I don't understand. Will there be any important messages in the envelopes?'

'Um, as I said, I'm not sure I'm the best one to explain. But come along with me to the post office and they'll tell you what to do next.'

The postman undertook to introduce me to his local postmaster.

'Ah, the white envelopes!' he exclaimed. 'I'm afraid to say we don't deliver those anymore. They've been re-routed to a special courier service.'

'But why?' I asked.

'They don't want their white envelopes to be mixed in with the rest of the envelopes.' he chuckled. 'I can refer you to their service for subscription if you really want, but you have to be aware that you won't receive anything other than their official, authorized envelopes. Their subscription specifically stipulates that you will completely cease the delivery of all other mail.'

I'm not sure why I felt compelled to explore this envelope thing further, but I had to admit that it had me intrigued. What was so special about these envelopes? Why could they come only through special courier? Why did I have to cease delivery of all other envelopes? It was different, mysterious. I wanted to discover more about these envelopes.

Most helpfully, one of the special couriers came to see me personally, when he heard I was interested in the envelopes. He explained that there was no contract, and no cost for the special courier service, or delivery of the white envelopes. I didn't even have to fill in any paperwork. Why not join up right away? It seemed harmless enough. I wasn't signing anything or relinquishing any money or rights, so I went ahead. A verbal agreement, and it was done. Maybe I could finally discover the secret of the white envelopes.

The white envelope delivery started almost immediately. I eagerly opened each one, only to be confronted with the same message - 'You know that this letter is correct because you got it from a white envelope delivered by special courier.' I tried to be patient, but felt I was ready for something more. I finally asked the special courier to come back and see me.

'Listen, I've been getting these white envelopes for a while, but I'm not getting any messages in them' I complained.

'There was nothing in the envelope at all?' he asked in surprise.

'Well, there was, but it just confirms that the letter is correct because it came in a white envelope by special courier. What's the real message?'

'But don't you see? The message is the envelope! The envelope is the message!' he exclaimed excitedly.

'How can the envelope itself be a message?' I asked. 'It's simply a mode of delivery, a device for holding a message. I'm not getting anything out of this.'

'You don't seem to be understanding the real spirit of this' he replied earnestly. 'You must try harder.'

The very next day, another envelope arrived. I wearily tore it open and read the same old message. Wait ... there was some fine print at the bottom of the page! It had never been there before. I squinted to read it. 'To ensure that you are worthy to keep receiving the white envelopes, it would be best if your mailbox had some work. The delivery slot is a little too small. Your mailbox does not appear to have been cleaned for some time, and we want to set a good example by having the cleanest mailboxes. It may also have escaped your attention that we prefer subscribed mailboxes to be white.'

Well, I had persisted this far. I guess I had to keep going. Maybe there would be more to the message once I got my mailbox cleaned up and made right. Maybe I could prove I was a worthy recipient of the white envelopes.

I cleaned my mailbox into tip-top shape. Scrubbed inside and out, and painted white. Each day I waited for an envelope, and felt a small thrill on the days when I opened the box and another one had finally come. I was still subscribed! As the days and weeks wore on, though, I noticed my box wasn't looking so great. The white showed the dirt badly. I seemed to be trying to clean it all the time. The more I cleaned it, the more I noticed the dirt the next time I checked it.

And while I was doing my best to have a clean mailbox, and keep all the envelopes collecting pristinely in my house, the small print at the bottom of each letter started to vary a bit more.

'Subscribers are reminded that they must not accept the delivery of any unauthorised envelopes.'

'Subscribers are warned to dispose of any unauthorised envelopes IMMEDIATELY without opening them.'

'Subscribers are warned that the contents of unauthorised envelopes may be dangerous.'

This did start raising some interesting questions in my mind. I looked for an opportunity to talk to the special courier again. I asked him about his concerns with other envelopes.

'You have to understand that our envelopes are plain and humble for a reason' he said. 'They are just like the first, original envelopes – white. We don't try to draw attention to ourselves with bright colours, or fancy designs and fonts. We remain the same, simple design as the very first envelopes – just plain white. You may think other envelopes are harmless, but the consequences for you could be dire. People have been led astray by other envelopes. They have received invitations to raucous gatherings. Their envelopes have been printed in a variety of gaudy colours and designs. They just seek to draw attention to themselves. Some envelopes even contain letters asking for money. And it is a very sad indictment on our contemporary society that many people do not see the connection between the envelope and the message inside. It's sad to say that some people just throw the envelope away without a second thought. We don't want this happening to our subscribers, so it is just much safer to avoid all other envelopes, and dispose of them immediately if any come your way.'

My old friend Ed came to visit. I hoped he wouldn't notice the envelopes, but he did.

'Hey, man, I don't want to be rude, but ... what's with the envelope collection? It looks like the Spanish Armada advancing on your lounge room from the sideboard.'

'They're – well – something I'm subscribing to at the moment.'

'Cool. What do they tell you? What's it about?'

'They're – uh – authorised envelopes. The same as the very first original envelopes that were ever used. They're about humility, and simplicity, and purity.'

'What's in them? What do you get inside? The meaning of life?'

'Yes, but – well the messages always point back to the envelopes. I guess it's more about the envelopes than what's in them. It's hard to explain.'

'Dude, that's a bit ...' he looked at me sideways.

'What?'

'Well, weird. I mean, isn't the whole point of an envelope the message it contains? If your envelopes always contain messages about the envelope they came in, isn't that a bit of a circular argument? I mean it kinda sounds like you're just chasing your tail.'

'The envelopes are ... about more than the envelopes! It's more like a new way of living. I get lots from it!'

'Like what?'

'Well, for one thing, I bet my mailbox is far cleaner than yours! And I always look forward to them.'

'Listen, man, whatever. I just think you're a bit obsessed with this envelope thing. Me, I prefer the banana to the banana peel. The chocolate to the wrapper. The birthday card to the envelope it came in. I love my coffee cup, but only because it holds coffee. I value my gifts more than their wrapping paper. If you're collecting special edition or first edition envelopes, then that could be cool, but these aren't them. They're just plain white!'

'Of course they're just plain white!' I said indignantly. 'The first envelopes were!'

'Actually, they weren't. The first prepaid wrappers used as envelopes were white, but they had a fancy design on them. The British Government held a special competition for someone to design what would become the very first officially used envelope, in the 1800s.'

'That's not true! It can't be true!' I shouted.

'Yeah, well, you're technically correct, but I was talking about the first PAPER envelopes. The VERY first envelopes were made of clay – the message was put inside on skin or whatever, and the damp clay crimped around it and baked hard. Pretty clever, really. You couldn't get the message without shattering the whole clay brick it was baked in. You always knew if the message had remained confidential.'

'Thanks for the history lesson, but you don't understand. These envelopes mean a lot to me.' I was upset now.

'Hey, easy, whatever floats your boat, man. I'm sorry, I'm not trying to sink your Armada ... wait, the British already did that. Ironic that we keep coming back to the British. Look, forget I said anything. At least you've got a back-up plan if you run out of toilet paper... sorry, that was insensitive. I think I might leave now.'

That week I had a visit from a pest inspector, and received some very bad news. I had white ants [termites]. The place was riddled with them. 'Severe structural damage, beyond repair' intoned the inspector mournfully. Or was it gleefully? The cost of house destruction and removal of the rubble would be immense, and would completely wipe out all savings. Worse, I'd still have the mortgage owing on the now non-existent house, while having to pay rent elsewhere. I could never afford to pay the mortgage, let alone get a new house. I was in despair.

When the courier came the next time, I was waiting at the mail box, and poured out my woes.

'Ah, it's not so bad' he said. 'Everyone has white ants to some extent. You can do away with most of them and get the rest under control.'

'You don't understand!' I wailed. 'My house is condemned. The council will be setting a date in the near future for destruction, and it's my responsibility to meet the cost! I'll be deeply in debt for a destroyed house, and will never be able to afford another one.'

'I have a secret for you' said the special courier as he leaned closer. 'WE KNOW HOW TO DEAL WITH THE WHITE ANTS!'

'Really? You do! That's … great! I won't have my house destroyed? How does it work?'

'These envelopes are all part of the process. They symbolise what is clean and white and pure and right and good. You've cleaned up your mailbox for them. But this is just the beginning. Now you can move on to getting the rest of your house in order. Clean everything. Whiten everything. Get rid of as many of the white ants as you can see, and then just keep painting white over everything, so that you won't see the ones that are still there.'

'That won't work' I said. 'The inspector will know I've still got white ants. The damage will still be there. The council will still destroy my house, because it's condemned!'

'No, no, people always overestimate the problem of the white ants' said the courier. 'If you try hard enough, you'll get rid of the worst areas, and the rest will look ok.'

'How will I make up for the structural damage?' I asked.

'That's not the point' said the courier. 'The inspector will see how hard you've tried. If it looks good enough, he just might accept it.'

'Might?'

'There are no guarantees, of course, that would be presumptuous. But if you do your best and it all looks as white as can be, that's all anyone can ask. And, of course, you must continue with your subscription without faltering. It will be a constant reminder of everything that is important – the need to just keep on going, and not quitting. Keep on with your subscription. Keep on trying to eradicate the white ants. Keep on with the whitening. Keep on keeping on!'

'About the envelopes ...' I began nervously. 'A friend of mine said that the first envelopes weren't just plain white ...'

'Why would you contradict what I've previously told you?' interrupted the courier angrily. 'Do you know how much effort I go to, bringing you these envelopes? Day in, day out? Sacrificing my life as an unpaid courier, bringing you these envelopes without cost? Have you not read every message that the envelopes have brought you? That the message is correct because the envelopes are white?'

'Yes, but, I'm just not sure why I wasn't told about the British Government's competition that...'

'That's quite enough.' The courier stood up to leave. 'You don't seem to appreciate your subscription. Perhaps you'd like it cancelled.'

'No, no!' I cried. 'Please, I want to continue my subscription. I want to get rid of the white ants. I need more whiteness in my life. Please don't leave me without the white envelopes.'

The following week I went out to check the mailbox. The courier hadn't been for a few days, and I was worried. I opened the box and my heart leapt into my throat. A BROWN ENVELOPE! I stared at it, just sitting there in my box, contaminating the whiteness. I was almost too afraid to touch it. Who had put it there? Why?! What would I do about it?! What if the courier saw it??!! That last thought brought me to my senses, and I snatched it out. Straight to the outside bin, I wouldn't even bring it into the house. There, gone. What a horrible incident.

A week later the same thing happened. Again, thank goodness I had seen it before the special courier delivery. I shuddered to think what would happen if he had come to deliver my mail and found an unauthorised envelope there. I put it straight in the bin again.

The third time, I carried it into the house and placed in on the kitchen table. What should I do about these deliveries? Maybe I should open just one and find out where they were coming from? Nooo! Don't open it! It's not white! I thought of all the warnings against opening unauthorised envelopes. It was probably a trick. A plant to catch me off guard, and prove I wasn't loyal to the subscription. Maybe it was delivered by a rival courier service or even the post office to entice me back to the general mail service. I finally sat it on my bedside table, out of sight of visitors and far away from the collection of white envelopes. I looked at it, but didn't open it.

The fourth week, the postman turned up at my door.

'What are you doing here?' I whispered furtively, glancing out towards the driveway, desperately hoping the special courier was nowhere in sight. 'I don't get your mail anymore!'

'Have you opened any of the brown envelopes?' he asked.

'Of course not! I mean, no, I've been kind of busy.'

'It's really important' he said. 'You must open one. It'll save your house from destruction.'

'That's ridiculous!' I retorted. 'Anyway, my house isn't going to be destroyed. It's all under control.'

'Please, just open it and read the message' he begged. 'You don't have to believe it or do anything if you don't want, but at least read it and then decide.'

I went to the bedroom and got the brown envelope. I brought it back to the door, opened it, and read it aloud.

'In the matter of termite infestation, all homeowners are invited to apply directly to the local council for full compensation of the destruction and removal cost of their condemned house. Furthermore, homeowners are guaranteed the reimbursement of all associated debt, and will be provided with a completely rebuilt home. All associated costs will be met by the council. Please lodge your claim at the nearest post office.'

I snorted.

'This can't be true. I mean it's all too easy. Why would the council pay for the removal of my damaged house, pay off its debt, and provide me with a brand new house?'

'They only give it to those who want it. You still have to go and apply' said the postman.

'But why? What's in it for them?' I asked incredulously.

'They understand the predicament you're in. They know no man can solve the white ant problem himself, and no one can undo the irreparable structural damage. The house must be completely destroyed and removed to eradicate the problem, and the cost is too high for people to meet. So it's an act of grace, I guess you could say.'

'But why haven't I heard of this before?' I asked. 'Surely if this were true I would have heard about it.'

'I guess you'd have to actually open and read the brown envelopes to know about it, wouldn't you now?' said the postman. 'Did you read the letters sent to you? Or did you ever try to find out what offers were available?'

He had me there. I hadn't investigated anything.

'There's just one problem' I said. 'The envelope is brown. Envelopes aren't supposed to be brown. How do I know that the message in it is true?'

The postman raised his eyebrows. 'You receive the best letter you're ever likely to receive, and you're worried about the colour of the envelope it came in?' he asked. 'If you ask me, you can't test a message by the envelope it came in. Test a message on its own merits – go and find out for yourself whether it's true!'

A few days later I crept in to the local post office. I stared at the vast array of postage packing in all shapes and colours. I looked at the different coloured envelopes and the bright postage stamps. I finally got up the courage to approach the counter.

'I, uh, got this brown envelope, and apparently I can apply for compensation for my condemned house here?' I asked hesitantly.

'You came to claim it! That's great!' He smiled at me broadly. 'Hand me your letter'.

I handed him the envelope and letter. He stamped the letter 'authorised', placed it in a folder and then crumpled my envelope in his hand before throwing it into the nearest bin. I stood completely still in shock for a moment, gaping at the waste bin and my crumpled envelope lying in it.

'That's – my envelope you just put in the bin.' I gasped feebly.

'What? Oh, sorry' he said. He reached in to the bin and took it out. He marched across the room and placed it ceremoniously into the recycling bin, and smiled. 'You're right, we should do better by the environment. You'll receive your confirmation in the mail soon.'

I stumbled home in confusion. The brown envelope had proven to be the bearer of my most important letter ever, and it was lying crumpled and discarded in some recycling bin. I didn't even have the letter that came in that brown envelope. I looked down at my empty hands. All I had was – the actual message itself. Not in any tangible form, but ... a promise. I went home and gazed at all my white envelopes on the sideboard. I gazed around at my white walls and floor and furniture. A white morgue full of tiny terminated and not-yet terminated termites. I wondered what the pest inspector would make of my eradication efforts if I tried to convince him that I had done enough to prevent the condemnation of my house. And I started to desperately hope that my confirmation letter would arrive from the council before the pest inspector showed up on my doorstep again.

I paced the house the following day, waiting for the postman. He finally came up the drive with a broad grin.

'Hey, a big manila envelope for you!' he cried. 'It looks very important.'

I tore it open in haste. My letter! It was here!

'The Council confirms that the house of the address noted above is granted full compensation for its destruction and removal, mortgage and full rebuilding.'

I was dancing a jig with the postman and didn't immediately notice the special courier making his way up the street. He stopped in front of me with a deep scowl as he noticed the envelope I waved in my hand.

'A MANILA ENVELOPE' he bellowed. 'MANILA!' Of all the things to lead you astray, this is the worst. I cannot possibly put a white envelope in your mailbox now that it's been contaminated in such a way.'

'Actually, that's ok!' I said cheerily. 'This is a special one-off envelope. I only need it once, and I don't think I'll need any white envelopes ever again.' I left him standing there and waltzed inside. I placed my letter carefully in the filing cabinet. I crumpled the manila envelope and threw it in the bin. I went into the lounge room and stared at the sideboard. Then I collected up all the white envelopes, one by one. It took several trips, but finally they were all in the bin. The recycling bin, I mean.

CPSIA information can be obtained
at www.ICGtesting.com
Printed in the USA
BVHW072313080622
639220BV00002B/263

9 780994 295309